PROLOGUE

Papua New Guinea (PNG) is a large island nation which lies directly north of Australia in the Western Pacific Ocean. I was surprised to note that it's the second largest island in the world after Greenland, (Australia being classed as a continent). Back in the 18th century, exploration of the Western Pacific ocean and the wider Pacific had captured the imagination of the whole of the developing world. News of Captain Cook's voyages of discovery in his ship the Endeavour were eagerly awaited year on year in Europe. At the time, there was no news report or article to match that of Cook's adventures, he was truly headline news. He and his crew first mapped and landed on New Zealand and Australia back in 1769. Others, like the Dutch explorer Abel Tazman had actually reported the sighting of New Zealand over a hundred years previously in 1642. From the time of Captain James Cook's voyages onwards however, colonisation in the Western Pacific became a consuming project for most of the developing world. Sailing ships were becoming capable of regularly circumnavigating the globe and their naval commanders were charged with discovering and claiming whatever they could for their homelands. From that time, and to this day in the 21st century, people from the developed world have emigrated to the area, resulting in Australia and New Zealand keeping close rank with the rest of the world in progress, technology and national prowess.

On the nearby Island of Papua New Guinea however, that second largest island in the world, colonialization and development was very slow to take place. For the island to remain so isolated through this intense period of exploration in the South Seas, there had to be reasons. The most obvious one would be the terrain in PNG which is very mountainous in places and accompanied by a wide covering of dense, impenetrable rain forest. One other reason may have been the reputation on the people native to PNG. They were a well-established people who fought among their own tribes at times and were accustomed to warding off anyone they saw as a threat. Some coastal areas and the large islands lying off the north coast of PNG were explored and exploited for mineral wealth as the 20th century advanced. Very few explorers ventured far in-land however until the 1950's. Tribes all over PNG lived their lives in their own ways, mostly completely untouched by the developing world. For them there was no iron age or bronze age, PNG remained firmly in the stone age throughout these eras and some areas remain so even to this day. Despite this ongoing isolation, not everything passed them by. Japanese, American and Australlian involvement in the second world war meant that battles raged all around the Pacific. This resulted in a lot of warfare in the skies above and in the seas around the island. For the inhabitants, this presented much amazement and mystery. Aeroplanes crashed into the island of PNG regularly throughout the war, we can only imagine what the tribes people must have thought. Wrecked cargos of merchant ships and battleships washed up on the shores. These events were interpreted in all sorts of ways by the native people. Some famous examples are the cargo cults where tribes often took to worshiping the items and artefacts which landed on their shores. In one example in the Sepic river region on the northern coast of PNG, a large quantity of shipwrecked items were assembled into a makeshift shrine. In some of the nearby island communities Prince Philip was worshiped as a god thanks to framed photographs of him often washing ashore from naval shipwrecks.

By the 1960's and 70's the inner and higher reaches of PNG were gradually being opened up to road transport. At that time a border was established directly north/south down the middle of the island and on the south east side lay Papua New Guinea under Australian and British control while to the north west, West Irian was under Dutch control. Germany had also colonised a large part of the island for a time in the late 19th century hence many of the German names still remained. Mount Wilhelm is the largest mountain in the Bismark mountain range and the Bismark sea lies off the north cost of PNG in the Western Pacific Ocean. As the 20th century advanced it became clear that the country would pass back into the hands of the local people. The days of claiming and keeping control of colonial territories were over, besides which neither the Australians or Dutch saw any real advantage in doing so. Many challenges lay ahead for the people of PNG, in trying to assimilate to a world which now prevailed around them. For young European and Australian people looking for true adventure in the early 1970's however, PNG remained a great place to go and live, work and explore. My parents were exactly such people, bringing up a young family in Scotland, but looking for adventure. They responded to an advertisement for teacing posts with the Overseas Development Agency in the *Edinburgh Evening News* and *Scotsman* newspapers at some point in 1972 and by January 1973 we were on our way.

WANPELA TAIM LONG PAPUA NIUGINI

Once Upon a Time in Papua New Guinea

For My Parents

CHAPTER 1 – "GUINEA PIGS"

"This is our flag, flag of our land, proudly it flutters and proudly we stand." As a boy I loved flags, I had a book with all the flags of the world in it. Occasionally I would draw little flags in the hallway of our home, hidden in the patterns of the wallpaper where I thought no one would notice them. This flag came to my attention like no other though, when I was nine years old. I came to love it and still do, there's not a flag anywhere which catches my eye the way this one does. It shows a bird of paradise and the Southern Cross star constellation, as anyone in Papua New Guinea will tell you and they too love their flag. For them it's a fitting symbol of their island & country, for me though it evokes a memory of an adventure to one of the most remote places imaginable. An adventure for my family many years ago and maybe also the ongoing adventure of the proud native people of Papua New Guinea. "Flag of our Island home in the sun, Papua New Guinea, we are one!" These are the lines of a popular national song sung in the Highlands of Papua New Guinea in the 1970's.

Like so many great adventures, this one started in a bath tub, in a town in Scotland in the winter of 1972. The days were short and cold. In the clear evenings the stars of the plough, Orion the Hunter and the Little Bear shone in the night sky. As children we often shared baths before bedtime and my brother and I, as ever in winter time, were never in any rush to get out of a hot bath. It required one or other of our parents to call an end to it and on this particular night our father walked into the bathroom. He sat down next to our bath and this night he had an aura, a look which told us something was afoot. For us sitting in the bath tub, that moment was the start!

What followed changed our lives, changed our outlook and left us with an experience like no other. *"Boys, we've just been telling your sister, we're going on an adventure, were going away on a long trip"*
"Where to dad?" we asked.
"We're going to Papua New Guinea" he said, as calmly as you can imagine.
"Guinea pigs, guinea pigs!" cried Roger as he chuckled and splashed.
"No, it's not to do with guinea pigs " he said, *"We're going to an island off the coast of Papua New Guinea called Manus island. It's near Australia in the Western Pacific,"* and I think he mentioned *"equator"* and *"it'll be very warm"*

I can remember that bath time as clearly as any moment in my life. I remember partly because of my younger brother Rog's mention of guinea pigs, he was only seven years old, but we knew right then this was big news. Looking back, life is fairly intense when you're nine years old, in the sense that new things fill your mind every day. I'd never heard of Papua New Guinea? As usual we were lifted from the bath and our heads & bodies dried with warm towels and sometimes we also had a spoon of malt syrup from the bathroom cabinet in the winter nights.

'My friends! How long are we going away for and what about the trials for the Burgh Primary School football team?' All kinds of questions came to us. *'Will they have football player cards for sale in Papua New Guinea?* My football card collection was only a few players from completion. All important questions and *'what was that about the equator?'* If we hadn't realised it coming out of the bathtub, we realised in the weeks which followed, this was more than just a trip. I don't remember the answer to the *"how long?"* question, our older sister Janet was 11 years old and just as eager to know. I think it dawned on us gradually but looking back, when it turns out you're heading to the other side of the world and a bit further, to Papua New Guinea, who could honestly say?
"Well your mother and I will have jobs there so it could be a year, maybe a year or two"

'Two years!' Some nights I couldn't sleep for thinking about it. *'Somewhere around November 1972. Surely we'll want to come home sooner?'* As it turned out, it was to be a two-year adventure of unimaginable discovery to one of the most remote places left on our planet, well out of sight from Orion the Hunter and the Little Bear.

The crate – *(part 1)*
The next few weeks leading up to the Christmas holidays were spent preparing for the trip. Telling friends, relatives and neighbours of our plans and seeing their surprise, sometimes sorrow at the news. They'd mostly never heard

of Papua New Guinea and for the grown-ups who've kind of heard of it, *"Where is it?"* It wasn't until many years later that my best friend of the time told me of being devastated at me going away. Then, amidst all this excitement and trepidation, a large crate appeared in our garage after school one day. The crate, the first real tangible sign of the trip. The crate seemed huge, around five feet high and around six foot square, with the wooden lid laid to one side. It was made of rough wooden slats and a source of splinters in fingers for curious children climbing up to see it filling up. I could have imagined a small car going in there at the time. It arrived a week or two before departure. Everything we needed, or thought we needed, was to go in the crate. All sorts went in there but no furniture, they'd have furniture for us at Manus Island. There would be a house for us at the school where our parents were going to teach and help manage the new education system. In went the record player, food mixer, blankets, lamps, garden tools, vacuum cleaner, golf clubs, Monopoly board game transistor radio and don't forget the cuddly toys!

I had only two or three things for the crate, my new leather football, from my birthday in October, my "Triang 70" bicycle and my large pack of football cards. The stack was now just one, maybe two players from completion but it was bigger than your hand could hold. John Greig was one of the missing players, he wasn't easy to get hold of. You'd have to swap several player cards, maybe ten or more, to get hold of John Greig if you hadn't been lucky enough to buy a pack with him in there. Some John Greig cards on offer were in such bad condition you'd wait for a better one. The crate was phenomenal, at least to me, my sister and brother. Eventually we saw it being nailed closed with six inch nails, bang, bang, bang and ready to go. As it turned out, it took a long, long time to reach us in our new home in Papua New Guinea.

"*Where did you say you're going.......?*"
"*We're going to Papua New Guinea!*"

CHAPTER 2 - DESTINATION MANUS ISLAND, WESTERN PACIFIC.

At the turn of 1973, the airport west of the city of Edinburgh had seen its best days, a large white building with clear signs of the art deco style from the time when it was built. Back then it was known as Turnhouse Airport and both the runway and the terminal lay in a different place to where they lie now. It had developed from an air force runway as our Dad explained but a new airport was coming soon. Back then we'd sometimes take a trip to the airport at the week-end just to watch the planes landing. There was a large open hall where you approached the check-in desks along the far side from the entrance and that seemed about all, no duty free, no restaurant as far as I can remember. Our family arrived there with three or four large suitcases, and tickets for connecting flights to London, Sydney, Australia and Port Moresby in Papua New Guinea.

The plan was ambitious, lots of flights lay ahead and we'd only ever been in an aeroplane once when our parents worked in Africa but we'd been too young to remember. It was very exciting to be at the airport. It always is but our mum's main concern was what type of aeroplane we'd board for the flight to London. Would it be a Trident? Of course we had no choice in this but I remember mum's concern when dad turned to her from the check-in desk, *"Trident"* he announced looking at her and smiling.

The BEA Trident aircraft was something to behold, it was fairly new to the airways. Air enthusiasts probably look back at it as something special but it had been in the news in the years before our departure for a couple of pretty catastrophic crashes. What stood out was its huge tail wings with a jet engine mounted on the tailpiece itself. As we soon realised, this allowed the Trident to take off at a very steep angle and to leave our mother's trepidation aside for now, it all seemed like the best of fun. As it took off you sensed yourself lying right back in your seat and even in the aisle seats you could sense the cabin floor sloping steeply up in front of you, those in the window seats could barely look out!

I dont know what actually became of the BEA Trident aircraft, I don't plan to look it up as no research at all is intended for these memoirs. I'd rather tell the adventure from my memory, the way I remember it happening as a nine and ten year old boy. What I can say, and aircraft enthusiasts will know better than I do, is that the Trident didn't last very long in service. We never flew in one or saw one ever again. The good news is that despite my sister, brother and I all having to use the sick bags, the Trident landed safely in London where we made our way to a bed & breakfast, ready for the next leg of our trip.

The next day, our connecting flight from London wasn't due to take off until late afternoon. For the Linton family this opened up a good opportunity, with an ambitious but truly fateful decision being made that morning to take the chance to go sightseeing in London. We went off to visit the Tower of London and saw the crown jewels. I think our Mum and Janet then went off shopping and our Dad took my brother and I on board a war ship moored on the Thames, HMS Belfast. We all met up after lunch to make our way across the busy London traffic for our trans global flight to Sydney Australia later that afternoon. We hadn't travelled a lot on aeroplanes and being the Linton family, instructions to arrive an hour or two early for a trans global flight were not taken seriously enough as it turned out. After making our way through London traffic I'm guessing we arrived at Heathrow Airport around half an hour before the departure time! We soon realised boarding was closed for the flight and despite our Dad's usual efforts to talk us out of trouble, our chances of catching our flight were nil! Arrangements were made to book us on the flight the next day and we went off for dinner and another night in a hotel nearer the airport, no further sightseeing planned for the next day as far as I remember.

The Boeing 737 was the main long haul aircraft back in the early 70's. Had it been night time we could have bid goodbye to Orion the Hunter and goodbye to the Little Bear. We'd heard of the 747 Jumbo, probably even seen one land on occasional trips to Turnhouse airport but we didn't have the good fortune to fly to Australia in the Jumbo. The trusty 737 on the other hand had two seats on one side of the aisle, three on the other. It soon felt a little cramped on the long haul to Australia and we stopped to refuel in both Bangkok and Singapore. We were able to get off the flight very briefly at both stops and we took the opportunity each time. Our seats were near the kitchen area towards the back of the cabin and the smell of aeroplane food together with being unaccustomed to flying meant I was airsick and unable to keep anything down on the entire flight to Sydney Australia.

Sydney Australia! We look a taxi from the airport to down town Sydney to a hotel on Bondi beach called the Astra Hotel. Of all the places, Bondi beach, and of all the hotels, the Astra Hotel! Some rest at last, and a good sleep in both the taxi and hotel. If you've never heard of the Astra hotel on Bondi, let me tell you it was quite a place to wake up in, at least it was in early 1973. I'd say it was about seven or eight floors high and sitting on top of it, above the whole Bondi skyline "Astra" in bright red letters which lit up at night. The restaurant was near the top floor and we were up early and very hungry after our travel ordeals.

The first thing of note on walking into the restaurant was a large table with rows and rows of glasses of orange juice. To me it tasted awful so we asked if they had the normal orange juice for the children?
"The normal orange juice love?"
"Yes the diluting juice"
"Diluting juice? .....Oh you mean cordial, you don't like the fresh orange juice? Sure we'll get ye some cordial love, no worries...no drama"
No drama? What about my football card collection? Incomplete and only two players short!
We sat at a table at the large windows delighted with our chosen cereal packs and *"cordial"* and *"no worries"* as we enjoyed our first settled meal in days. Outside, from the panoramic window Bondi beach was coming to life.
"There are people swimming out in the waves Dad, over there!"
"They're early morning surfers son, they're out before it gets hot and crowded. Its summertime here as I was telling you."

Its summertime! Two days travelling in aeroplanes and suddenly it's going to be blazing hot today. I'm fine with a new name for orange juice, fine with the Coco Pops but summer time, how can that possibly be? The surfers paddled patiently on their boards, maybe half a dozen or a dozen of them and then at last a spell of bigger waves.

Wow! Up they got onto the boards, surfing along the like something you'd never imagined then right into the wave tunnels like you really wouldn't believe! Breakfast time at Bondi Beach, cordial, coco pops, surfers and summertime, and for the time being, no worries at all.

We spent the day at the beach, a full day's rest before flying north. Bondi beach is a beach filled with Aussie people and Aussie life. We needed swimming "cozzies" and sun tan lotion, lots of it. Aussie beach life, volleyball, Bondi hot dogs, picnics and cold beers, Aussie rules and Aussie language. *"Bloody flies, get the Aero-guard! ....little bastard's, don't spray the bloody hot dog!"* Very different from beaches in Scotland and hard to believe this all goes on. *"Bloody bute"* and *"Christ!, Jesus H Christ..?"* As the tide went out people set up volley ball courts and played hand tennis and all manner of beach games. *"bloody ball was out mate, fair dinkum!".... "fair dinkum?"* Some people were throwing boomerangs out across the water then running to catch them as they turned round high in the air and came flying back. You never forget your first day on Bondi beach, and the surprise when other kids tell you "*you're a pommie!*"

The next day we flew from Sydney to Brisbane and we waited in Brisbane airport for a few hours for our connecting flight to Port Moresby, capital of Papua New Guinea. It was getting warner as we headed north and we were complaining a bit during the wait for the next flight. Some people next to us in the waiting lounge were from Darwin at the north tip of Australia, or *"Dar'n"* as the guy pronounced it. *"Jesus it's bloody freezin' in Brisbane love"* he was saying to his wife. As we'd already learned on the beach at Bondi, Aussies loved to have a joke at the pommie's expense.

One of these flights was in a Boeing 727, possibly both of them. We were getting to know the Boeing aircraft fleet, it was one of the few things of interest to read in the back of the seat in front. I don't think we were air sick on the leg from Brisbane to Port Moresby and only four or five hours to endure. Port Moresby, the capital of Papua New Guinea lies in a bay in the south east corner of the island, a bit north of Dar'n. I wouldn't be surprised if Dar'n broke right away from Moresby away back in time and drifted south, but that's just a wild guess. Descending into Port Moresby we flew along the coastline and groups of large and small palm trees appeared and lined the roads in places. As we came to know, they were coconut and banana palms among others, but all completely new to us.

Port Moresby wasn't a big city, more like a large town town at the time and without much warning, we'd landed. *"Welcome to Port Moresby, thanks for flying with Quantas"* Within minutes of arriving on the tarmac the cabin started to feel really hot, we couldn't wait to get into the fresh air. The steps from the Boeing 727 had a canvas type canopy over the walkway and between the walkway and the aeroplane doorway, there was a small gap in the canopy. The blast coming through the gap on exiting the aeroplane was something I'll never forget. It was difficult to come to your senses, what was that superheated blast as we alighted the plane? Then as we stepped onto the tarmac there was the realisation, it was the Port Moresby breeze. There would be no cool fresh air outside the cabin. Hence our first thoughts on setting foot in this completely new place were how can anyone tolerate this type of heat?
"It's like hair drier blasting us!" we were saying and it was, like a huge invisible hair drier blowing on us and dry-

ing our mouths. We then arrived in some air conditioned buildings where the staff confirmed it was always this hot but also *"a bit humid today."* I'd never even heard of "humid" until that day in Port Moresby.

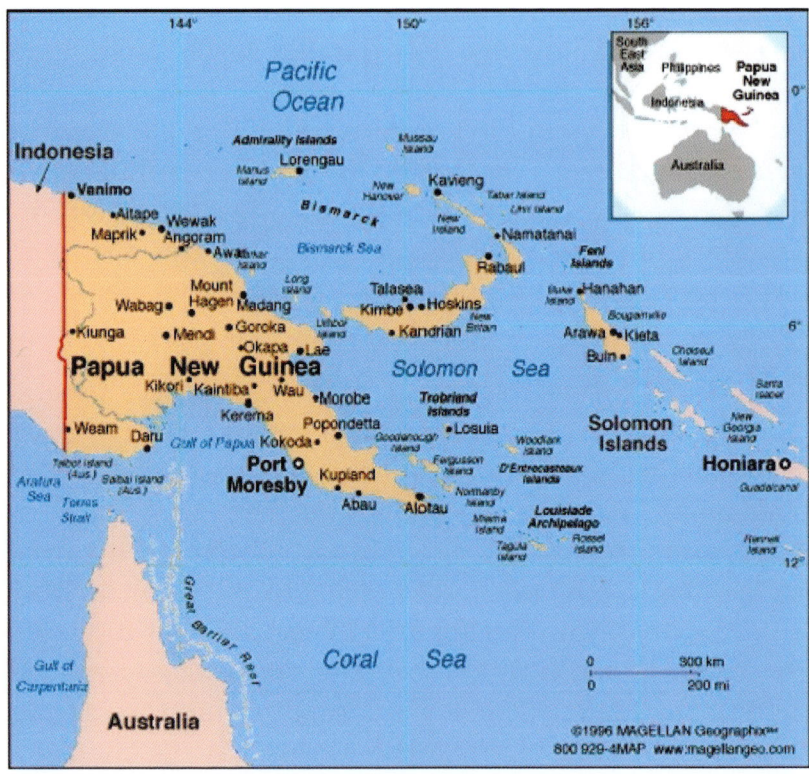

One thing we'd learned about Papua New Guinea from being shown it on the world atlas, it lies right above Australia but it also lies just under the equator. So that's the equator, *a line round the middle of the world for the closest point to the sun*. Having also managed to pinpoint tiny Manus Island before we left Scotland, we knew it lay north of PNG even closer to the equator, in fact very close indeed. You can see it on the map, right at the top of the island archipeligo which stretches north above the main island of PNG. In the short time taken to get to the education building you can imagine our thoughts: *This is a very hot place we've arrived in, really unbearably hot but what about Manus Island, it's going to be even hotter!*

We had arrived in the tropics, tired & overwrought in the education building on Port Moresby. PNG was still an outpost of the British empire in 1973 and still governed by Australia so the people we met initially were quite familiar to us We were also thinking we were getting near our destination now but as it turned out the trip was about to take a completely unexpected turn.

We had a long wait on some seats outside the meeting room but with one saving grace, air conditioning. The first time you experience air conditioning there's a real strange sensation, like walking into a refrigerator. After five or ten minutes, you start to realise it's not cold and it's just the normal temperature you're used to, there's just a huge contrast with the temperature outside in Port Moresby. Eventually our dad reappeared from the meeting room and he's looking straight at our mum.
"The headmaster job in Manus Island is taken Mary, it's no longer available."
"It's what?"
"The position is taken"

You'd be quite right now if you're thinking back to that day out in London. London town, old and new, see the sights, and the sales! The tower of London, a fun place and the crown jewels, the yeomen and the ravens. HMS Belfast is a cracking ship but what a turn events had now taken as a result of missing our flight that day. It's good to have the air conditioning though, that's for sure as it's unbelievably hot outside in Port Moresby. It may have been down to us having left London a day late then ended up a few more days late from our travels or it may have been the way overseas airmail letters travelled slowly in 1973 but whatever the explanation, the teaching posts in Manus Island were no longer available. As kids, it was difficult for us to know what to think now, except maybe it would be good to fly back to Australia and tell that guy how bloody freezin' it is back in Dar'n! We were all bewildered and disappointed at the news and yet our parents still seemed to be keeping up a brave face. They'd come all the way across the world, to Papua New Guinea, with their three children and now the posting in Manus Island had slipped away. Most of our supplies and belongings were in a crate somewhere at sea, on a slow boat to PNG addressed to the Linton Family, Manus Island.

To or great relief, some better news followed. It soon became apparent that the Papua New Guinea education department would definitely be happy to accommodate us in some way or other. Maybe we should never have doubted it but given what lay ahead. A new offer came into view before we left the education building that day, a post in the Western Highlands, Chimbu District. Some more good news, apparently it's much cooler in the highlands. We'd be many thousands of feet up in the Chimbu District and *"the climate is much cooler but still quite humid"*.

I guess we couldn't say at this point if this was a lucky break or whether we missed out on a tropical paradise out in the Bismark Sea but whatever Manus Island may have had in store, we had now changed course. Chimbu District in the Highlands of Papua New Guinea was said to be just over one generation from the stone age. It bordered on large areas of the Western Highlands as yet unexplored or recorded. Within a few hundred miles of our new destination, head hunters still roamed the rain forests and river deltas. Entire tribes had never come into contact with anyone other than their enemies up or down stream and cannibalism was not unknown.

The Civic Guest House, Port Moresby – we arrived there that evening, courtesy of the Papua New Guinea education authority. The end of a long and notorious day was drawing near. I can only guess at our dad's parting comments at the education building: *"Oh and by the way, there will be a large wooden crate arriving here in Moresby sometime soon addressed to the Linton Family, Manus Island, please redirect it to Kerowagi High School, Chimbu District when it arrives."* Could we not just have stayed at Bondi? There had been shocks to the senses and blows to our plans and yet there were still more surprises lying in wait, even in the comfort of the Civic Guest house.

We lay in our beds in a large family room in the Civic Guest House with our parents in the outside bar tables having a drink or two taking stock of events that day. We could hear occasional loud bangs in the roads nearby as coconut pods fell from the palm trees in high summer. It was then we became aware of some deep buzzing sounds in the room. As our eyes became used to the darkness, we could see them starting to move on the ceiling. Monsters! Still known to this day as the monsters! In our terror at seeing these creatures on the ceiling, the unthinkable happened, they started to dive bomb from the ceiling towards our beds. We dived out from under our bed sheets I ran towards the door and the open air corridor which led straight out to the poolside tables. At this point a truly memorable and notorious thing occurred. My sister Janet then abruptly closed the door behind me leaving me out in the corridor and shouted *"Get Mum and Dad!"* from inside the bedroom where she stayed looking after Rog. Of all the things going on, one of us having to venture out to the outdoor bar wearing pyjamas was clearly the scariest task. It stands to reason I suppose, I'd never been outdoors in pyjamas and never in a bar. I stepped out from the corridor, just visible to people in the bar and beckoned to our parents in a loud whisper *"Mum, Dad, there's monsters, monsters in the room!"* They turned out to be large cicadas, insects which become active at night easily ten times larger than any insect we'd ever seen. They're very common in Papua New Guinea and as we later learned, they're kept out of houses in the evenings using wire window netting. Once they do get in though, they're very difficult to chase out. They can be illusive and fairly indestructible. We all slept close packed in two beds and fell off to sleep exhausted.

There's little more to tell you about Port Moresby except that we stayed at the Civic Guest House for nearly a week as plans were laid for our ongoing journey. It was terrific, they had a nice swimming pool and we swam there all day, more swimming than we'd ever done in our lives. Freestyle, breast stroke, backstroke, in between trying to drown each other. We learned to swim breadths, then lengths of the pool and finally swim a whole length underwater.

CHAPTER 3 - DESTINATION CHIMBU DISTRICT, WESTERN HIGHLANDS

As far as I know there are two main types of aeroplanes. Two types back then and still to this day, jet planes and propeller planes. There would be no more Boeing jets on our journey north from Port Moresby, the next plane we boarded was called a Twin Otter. Our Dad had pointed out another plane called a Fokker Friendship on the tarmac at Port Moresby airport, one he'd hoped to travel in but not on this occasion. "Fokker Friendship" what a great name for an aircraft, I've never forgotten it, who would? The noise of the Twin Otter propellers as it started up and taxied to the runway was deafening! Do they need to be so noisy before the trusty Twin Otter even takes off? Can the famous Fokker Friendship be as noisy as this? Well we may not have been flying in the Fokker but by now no-one cared, the Twin Otter turned out to be fantastic. On its side and on the headrests of the chairs was emblazoned TAA – Trans Australian Airlines.

Destination Goroka, first and last major town on the way into the highlands of Papua New Guinea in January 1973 and the Twin Otter starts its charge down the Port Moresby runway. None of the exhilarating thrust of the jet planes where you're abruptly pinned back in your seat, just noise, much more noise and a lot of shaking, *have we taken off yet?* These propeller planes were a completely different flying experience. Once airborne and when the racket and vibration begins to die away, it's something else alltogether. Every turn and tilt of the plane you can feel and every buffet of wind, every climb and fall. When you combine the novelty on this type of flying experience with the truly startling views from the windows of the plane, out to the highlands of New Guinea the drama only starts to dawn on you. The hillsides are terraced here and there so the natives can farm the steep hillsides and so steep you'd never think it possible. Small villages appear almost anywhere, in valleys, on small plateaus and half way up hillsides. The houses are small, round and have roughly thatched roofs. They're made from nothing more than the trees, bamboo and grasses which surround them and they blend with the hillsides and valleys in a simple and perfect way. Small slicks of smoke rise from the houses and villages here and there.

Do people really live this way? ...and do people really live here on these hillsides? The hills rose sharply up towards the Twin Otter as it twisted and turned its way through the skies and the slopes then fell away just as suddenly. Compared to the dry coastal plains of Papua to the south, it's suddenly very green. Hills covered in jumbled trees and bushes in all shades of green and deep dark valleys with rivers and waterfalls tumbling through them. White wispy clouds lay deep in the valleys and clung to the lower hillsides. Nothing you'd ever seen could compare to it. The climb into this scenery was steep, engines roared then hummed as the Twin Otter probed and picked its way into the highlands but it never rose far above the scene below. I can't remember if there was a toilet, there may have been but there was no cabin crew. The flight crew consisted of the pilot and co-pilot up front with passenger seats right in behind them. No seat belt signs went on and off, you kept your seat belt on all through the flight. Those sitting near the cockpit could see all the controls clearly. The pilot flicked switches and passed messages to his co-pilot and pulled and pushed the joystick as he flew the plane high into the mountains and deep into the highlands. A regular conversation went on all through the flight between the two smartly dressed men with their TAA badges on their shirts & hats.

The descent to Goroka was the least pleasant part of the flight. Something not encountered as yet on our journey was the intense earache you can feel in unpressurised aeroplane cabins. It was at its worst on descent and no amount of chewing gum or sucking sweets was helping. We later learned a very useful trick of regularly holding your nose and blowing into the ear canals to equalise the pressure on the many flights which followed during our time in PNG.

Goroka was an impressive town. We didn't realise it on our first visit there but it would come to signify a step back towards normal civilisation to us in the times ahead. We took a taxi to the Minagere Hotel where we stayed overnight. The streets were quite broad and well laid out. There were shops and mini bus services and people all generally wore clothes. It may seem strange to mention but Goroka was the last place on the journey where the natives tended to wear western clothes. There was an open top restaurant in a hotel in the main street where you could have lunch. Goroka still had a colonial feel to it. The busy shops sold many things we'd not really encountered before. It was in Goroka where our parents realised it was time to buy more shorts and colourful T shirts so we'd fit in a little better, and open flip-flop shoes. I think our dad looked into buying a car in Goroka, which he would return to pick up some time later.

The Minagere Motel was great. It had a large swimming pool where guests spent most of their time. It was here that we realised there was a choice of two soft drinks in New Guinea, in common with most colonial places, Fanta & Coca Cola, in ice cold bottles. Goroka was noticeably cooler than Port Moresby. It was very hot at midday when we went for lunch but by now we all had hats. The Minagere Motel also had air conditioning and cereal packs at breakfast like the Astra, a terrific place and one we were to return to more than once.

Leaving Goroka felt a bit like leaving everything we may have still held dear. For one thing, we were about to board the smallest and last aeroplane on our journey. The sixth plane since starting in the Trident would now take as on to the town of Kundiawa. It was called a Cessna and had room for our family, two other passengers and the pilot. It had one propeller on the front and presented yet another extreme step in flying experiences. The Twin Otter had been exhilarating, flying up and down through the valleys, but now there was the Cessna. Seriously!... flying like a very noisy bird, up and down in the draughts, engine roaring then dying, climbing, floating and literally falling. On we flew, through banks of clouds and along tighter and steeper valleys, on into the Western Highlands. The town of Kundiawa had something called an "airstrip", not an airport. Flat places for landing aeroplanes were clearly more and more difficult to come across but the airline companies improvised in whatever way they could. The western highlands were more rugged than anything we'd seen so far with more rain forest, rivers and torrents cut deep alleys into the mountains. Depending on conditions and your pilot's approach to things, Kundiawa airstrip could be approached by aircraft from below, or just above. Not kidding, no drama, you flew between the hillsides towards runway which was short in length and fell away completely at one end. The Cessna flew gradually up towards the airstrip then the pilot cut the engine back and landed the little plane, plonk! Although we hadn't vomited since the London to Sydney flight, we vomited again now, and right into our new hats! TAA Cessna flights didn't supply sick bags, come to think of it there hadn't been a safety demo either.

Welcome to Kundiawa, bring your hats filled with vomit you're all welcome in Chimbu District, the new frontier! Kundiawa, a small town in the highlands of Papua New Guinea and it makes an immediate impression. We walked out from the airstrip building onto the upper section of the main street and most of the town can be seen from this vantage point. As we'd discover there was a supermarket from the Steamships company, some other shops, called "trading posts" and houses built on stilts with tin roofs. Kundiawa was where we'd attend school, at Kundiawa primary "A" school. The town sits in quite a tight spot in the Waghi river valley near where the Waghi river meets the Chimbu river and stretches up the surrounding hillsides. It's organised in places but a highland out post compared with Goroka. You can be forgiven for thinking we've reached journeys end now, but not yet. We still need to get to Kerowagi and we're not stopping long in Kundiawa as someone from Kerowagi has come to meet us, someone with an open backed truck.

Weeks of journeying are almost at an end but for a 17 mile trip along the Chimbu Highway in an large blue open backed truck with benches along each side at the back and railings to hold onto. The most striking thing now is the people, we're back on terra firma, with the people all around us. Some people were encircling our truck and taking a very close look at us. The natives of the highlands wear grass skirts, nothing on their feet and my brother Rog is now nudging at me smiling from ear to ear. "*Boobies!*" he's saying. The native girls and ladies wear nothing but grass skirts.

By this point in our journey and for the first time, things became a little overwhelming. The natives were friendly, as many an explorer has stated, but they seemed as fascinated with us as we were with them and also a little scary. It was good to move off out of town in the truck but the novelty was gradually replaced with fatigue and the discomfort. The Chimbu Highway was under construction and it degenerated quickly a few miles out of Kundiawa. Where the stony road surface has been "graded" and flattened the truck makes good headway but in many places the road is no more than a mountainous stone track. You're having to hold on tight as you're thrown around in the back of the open truck and on and on the journey goes.

The truck moved in and out of every gear as it navigated the mountain highway. In and out of small villages and settlements and eventually to the Mingende catholic mission station. Somewhere to stop for a toilet and a drink, half way from Kundiawa to Kerowagi and we're pretty much exhausted. On the second half of the trip came the full realisation of where we'd come to. What we saw as civilisation was now gone, no longer around us. These were the only recently explored highlands of Papua New Guinea and it hadn't actually been our intended destination. It wasn't Manus island, in the Bismarck sea, but this was where we found ourselves.

Villages came and went with small groups of native people staring fascinated at our open backed truck. Most were dressed in their grass skirts and women and men alike all topless with bare feet. Some of the small groups danced and shouted as we passed. We'd seen plenty of these villages from the air as our Cessna had climbed through the mountains but they appeared a little less idyllic as we passed through in our truck. Small clusters of bamboo huts appeared where there were clearings in the forests. The wisps of smoke still rose from the grass roofs and you could see the woven patterns of the hut walls. The woven bamboo was called "pit-pit" as we later learned, the natives used bamboo to build everything, they even stripped the bamboo bark to lash it all together.

Finally, we turned off the Chimbu highway leaving the only main road behind, to make its own way into the Western Highlands of New Guinea. We turned right at the Koronigl bridge and up the stony and very uneven road along the side of the Koronigl valley towards our new home. About half way along the three or four mile stretch from the highway, the road veers away from the river and up to a plateaued area of land where sits the small town of Kerowagi. We were relieved, I think, to find Kerowagi to be more than a collection of bamboo huts and surprisingly well laid out considering the half broken road which brought us north from the highway. From first impressions, many of the houses had tin roofs and windows, including ours as it turned out. As you enter the town, to the left of the main road is dominated by Kerowagi High School and to the right, Mr Heagey's store the single trading post in town. As the main road bends left towards Mengagl, you can turn right along a short road towards the airstrip or continue to one more right turn where the road is dotted with more houses, continue past the hospital and eventually to the Kiap's house at the top of the hill.

Kerowagi, Chimbu District, around 6000 feet altitude as I came to realise. Much higher than the highest mountain in the UK and still very warm through the day but cooler than Port Moresby as promised by the PNG education board. We've come all the way round the world. It's not Manus Island, we're exhausted from gripping onto the rails of the truck, but we're going no further, welcome to Kerowagi.

CHAPTER 4 - KEROWAGI

In the days and weeks after our journey across the world, we went about the task of acclimatising ourselves to the Western Highlands of New Guinea. Very little in the surroundings bore any relation to anything back home in Scotland. There was barely a tree or a flower you'd recognise. Most trees in the highlands are either bamboo or tropical pine trees and dense vegetation and jungle prevailed an all areas which hadn't been cleared for settlements. No oak trees, beach trees, chestnuts or sycamores which we knew from pressing their leaves in the pages of our school books back home. The low hedge along the front of our garden was poinsettia, common a few decades later as an ornamental indoor plant in the UK but used to form beautiful bright red leafed hedges all around where we lived.

Our house was very different from anything we were used to. Like all the houses in the school compound and the better houses in the town, it was built on stilts around two feet off the ground. The roof was made of corrugated iron and the walls were made of plywood sheeting. The most obvious feature though, was louvered windows right along the length of the house on both sides. These features made for a house which could be kept cooler in the hot season and dry in the rainy season. Yes, the rainy season, another thing to try to get to grips with was no spring, no summer or autumn, just one long hot season and a short rainy season. Along the front of the long sections of louvered windows there was close fitting wire netting which did a good job of keeping insects out of the house. In the evenings, large clusters of cicadas *("monsters")* clung to the wire netting, attracted by the lights of the house. They made a harmonious buzzing sound, not unlike the sound crickets make but a much lower pitched, like the base section of the insect orchestra.

At the south end of our house were two very large water tanks, just shorter than the height of the house itself. All the water which landed on the roof during the rainy season accumulated in these tanks. This then became our water supply right through the ten month dry season. By the end of the dry season during our second year, the tanks ran dry but we were able to top them up with water from some unoccupied houses on the compound using buckets and a ladder. When we first moved in we spent unlimited time in the shower but still not long as the water wasn't heated. Then as our parents realised the tank levels were dropping, shower times dropped to one minute and eventually around thirty seconds. Not kidding, try it some time it can be done! When the rain finally came again, we went out into the garden to dance around in the downpour, as the rain slowly made its way back into the parched ground. The rain came in fits a starts over a couple of days then stayed, almost constant for a month or two.

A very large garden came with the house. We were right at the north edge of the school compound bordering the road which ran through Kerowagi. At the western edge of our garden, the land fell away down a hillside towards the Tem Creek. The hillside was covered mostly with a banana plantation when we arrived and you could smell the bananas quite strongly as they began to ripen. They also planted a large field of sugar cane down nearer the road later in our stay. A gang of men came and smashed through the sugar canes with machete knives all day long when it came to the harvest. If you picked a good time, a guy would chop a section of sugar cane and pass it to you. It was the sweetest most refreshing thing, the sugar syrup flowed out from the stringy flesh inside the cane as you chewed into it.

We had a large vegetable patch planted out in plots at the end of the garden nearest the road. Until that time, we didn't know that if you chop the top off a pineapple and plant it in the ground with plenty of water, the spiked leaves grow into a spikey bush. Then the next pineapple comes right up through the middle and you wait until it's ready. We also didn't know that monkey nuts (pea nuts) grow under the soil. When you plant them, give them plenty water and a small very low level bush appears. After a few months you dig down and there are the monkey nuts, the root of the pea-nut plant under the soil.

The Kerowagi High School compound where we were provided our house was well laid out, probably better laid out than anywhere for miles around. It was an organised collection of school buildings, teachers houses and large dormitories segregated for male and female students with three of four dorms in each case. It occupied an area totalling around a dozen sports grounds, including the sports ground itself. The pupils came from the more organised families in a rapidly developing country and came from all over the Western Highlands. Some came from nearby towns some from remote villages far and wide but all of them came from families determined to send them to Kerowagi for their education. It was the largest secondary school in the Western Highlands, chosen for it position between Mount Hagen and Kundiawa. Its catchment area ran for forty or fifty miles in all directions

The small outpost town of Kerowagi was built on one of the few appreciable plateaus on the higher ground in the district. The rest of the area featured steep hillsides and deep valleys. In the mornings, clouds gathered everywhere, filling the valleys and appearing in banks along the hillsides. Whenever you had a vantage point in the early morning in Chimbu district, the scenery rolled out beautifully before you with the mists and clouds accompanying the sunrise. Kerowagi was bounded by the white water Koronigl river to the east and the smaller but steep valley of the Tem creek to the west. The terrain fell away south towards the highway and rose sharply to the north into the spectacular Bismark mountain range. The veranda of our house looked north into these mountains, the first of which was an imposing flat topped mountain. Our mother enjoyed reading on the veranda and the mountain became known to us as Mum's mountain. It was inevitable we'd climb this mountain but on only one occasion I can remember. Just like back in Scotland, it was advisable to let people know you were out hill climbing, but not so much for concerns about weather, more in relation to the mood of native tribes, which could change from day to day.

Other than the dramatic scenery around the remote town on Kerowagi, the most notable feature was the airstrip. It lay to the west of the town, just above the river valley and was serviced by a small airport building, no bigger than our house, which also served as the post office. The airstrip itself was grass sufaced, not tarmac. Small planes flew in from the south and unlike in Kundiawa, it was possible to descend onto the airstrip in the more traditional way. Landings were not frequent at Kerowagi, often weeks apart and were always greeted by small crowds of native people often coming from many miles away to see an aeroplane landing. They cheered and danced from first sight of the small Cessna planes flying up the valley, to the point when they landed and taxied to a halt. Passengers descending onto the grassy airstrip were greeted with yet more cheering, ayeee, ayeee! The airstrip was a real life line bringing vital air-mail deliveries among other things which couldn't be safely transported by road or track. Kerowagi High School and the airstrip were the most important features of the town, emerging in the remote western highlands of Papua New Guinea in 1973 but there were other features which were vital to people who'd settled there and of rapidly increasing importance to the native tribes people.

Heagney's store sat on the right hand side of the road just after you enter the town from the highway. The shop sold bottled and tinned goods, electrical appliances, mainly radios, farming tools and a small selection of sweets. Outside the shop on the stony forecourt stood a large free standing pump from which Mr Heagney sold petrol. I couldn't have imagined a more fascinating piece of equipment as a young boy. The petrol pump was of an old fashioned design rarely ever encountered in PNG or anywhere else. On its side was a large handle and on the top, just above head height was a large bowl shaped glass reservoir marked with some graduations. When you asked for a quantity of petrol, Mr Heagney unlocked the big handle and began pumping the amber coloured petrol up into the reservoir until almost full. He then released the contents through the filler hose into the petrol tank and I'd watch in fascination as he repeated the process two or three times.

We also bought a new radio from Mr Heagney's store. It would be a while before our crate of possessions would arrive from Scotland and besides, we needed a good radio to pick up the World Service on the short wave frequency. The world service only broadcast at certain times of the day and mostly broadcast news & current affairs. In the mornings we listened to the world news and at the end of each news bulletin there was an episode of the Wombles of Wimbledon. *"Under ground, over ground Wombling free, the*

Wombles of Wimbledon Common are we." It was as we were listening to one of these episodes one morning when we first experienced an earth tremor or "guria" as they were known in PNG. We were suddenly aware of a ting-ting-ting noise as some glasses and plates in the kitchen started taping together. It grew to a louder ting-ga-ting-ga-ting-ga sound and we were aware if the floor vibrating a little. As it continued our parents mentioned that this was an earth tremor and that these things did happen in PNG. It continued for around thirty seconds to a minute and we were relieved as it died away. It didn't affect the radio though, Madame Cholet and Uncle Bulgaria wombled on throughout. We experienced quite a few gurias some of greater magnitude than others but they only ever lasted a few minutes at the most. On one occasion we had to pull over on the highway because the car was moving around on the road. Once we'd stopped and looked ahead you could see the stones skipping around on the road and in the distance the road looked like it was shaking, with wave motions moving along its length.

On the road from Mr Heagney's store to the south end of the airstrip there was a building which sometimes served as a pub. It was a simple hut type building with tin roof, no windows and about half the size of our house. The locals were given permission for a pub there but every time it opened for business, trouble broke out within a week or two and the police and Kiap would be called up. Locals would sometimes fall out of the door and fights broke out fairly regularly. This would result in the pub being closed and curiously, it often went on fire soon afterwards. They fixed it up the next year and it reopened, only for a very similar chain of events to repeat itself, including the fire. At home in Scotland we actually see a similar pattern at times with some of our pubs, the only difference being they tend to open for a few years at time rather than a week or two at the most in Kerowagi.

At the highest point of the town, to the North, sat the Kiap's house. The Kiap was appointed by the newly formed local authority as it was at the time, to keep order in the town. Resident in the Kiap's house at the time were the late Mr Bill Graham and his wife Joan, who'd arrived in PNG from Northern Ireland a couple of years before us. The stony track road ran past the Kiaps house and back down to the north end of the airstrip. Also at the top end of the town sat the Ex-patriots Club, known to all ex-pats in Kerowagi as "the club". The club opened mostly at weekends, it was a large round building mirroring those built by the natives as meeting houses and constructed of similar woven bamboo walls and grass roof. Inside there was a bar, a projector and screen for showing movie reels, table tennis and eventually, a pool table.

Outside there was a fairly flat tarmac tennis court and a somewhat disappointing swimming pool. It was a pool built with rough concrete sides and filled by diverting the small local stream along a channel when the stream was running well. It was rumoured that the local villagers used it for washing and bathing during week days and hence it was off limits at times and needed to be regularly drained and cleaned. On the occasions when the pool was cleaned, the stream was diverted in along corrugated iron sheets towards the pool but the natives would often re-divert the stream leaving the pool only partly full and rightly so looking back, it was their stream after all. The stream was the lifeline for their crops and bathing and everyone knows what it's like to wake up one morning with no water supply! Some epic tennis matches took place between our parents and their friends, the club was a smashing place where we went every Saturday and usually stayed into the evening.

Movie reels arrived with the airmail every few weeks amidst great excitement, in the form of two flat metal movie cans containing the reels. The chairs were all re-assembled for movie night and each reel was then projected onto a large white screen opposite the bar. Changing over to the second reel made for a natural break where everyone topped up their drinks from the bar then settled down for the remainder of the movie. These movies were a real treat as you can imagine. The most memorable movie for me was the Italian Job with Michael Caine with the mini cooper cars making off with the stolen gold bullion. It gave us a glimpse of the fasionable cars of the time back in Europe and many stunts driving through the city and up into the hills. I cant say I remember every stunt as I've seen the movie too many times since that night but the ending I do remember from the time as the bus balanced on the precipice after very nearly skidding off the road *"Right lads, I've got an idea!"*

At the bar there was a choice of Coca Cola, Fanta and bottles of SP beer (South Pacific Brewery) which our parents and the rest of the guys drank when cold but they didn't speak highly of it. The Aussies had a nick name for SP beer, *"stinkin piss"*! Martini and Cinzano I also remember grown ups drank with great delight, all thanks to the *"excellent standard of living"* The club was a real hub for social contact among the ex-patriot community, the only drawback being the local tribes people took delight in robbing the contents during the week on a fairly regular basis. Better and better security seemed to inspire the natives to more and more audacious robberies!

Kerowagi Ex-patriots Club, 1973

Driving back down the hill from the Club, the stone track wound its way past the few expat houses occupied by people who worked outside of the school compound. On the left you passed the public works yard where two or three very sturdy open backed trucks were kept and maintained, including the one which brought us to Kerowagi on our first arrival. The road then passed the marketplace which was an area the size of a couple of tennis courts with some basic shelter and rough wooden benches. Finally, the road straightens out as it reaches more level ground where it passes the hospital and a small building containing the power generator. The hospital was small but of more modern construction like the school houses and the Store. I remember once seeing a young native boy being carried into the hospital with a wooden barbed arrow protruding from his leg during the tribal conflicts. He was barely conscious and it appeared his co-warriors had carried him a fair distance from where the Siku and Gena tribes were waring over land being developed for coffee plantation.

Kerowagi village market didn't look like much at all when passing it on the road but on market days it could be a real experience. Open air food markets have a buzz the world over I'd say and the little market in Kerowagi was no different. The natives brought whatever excess produce they had from their terraced farms which hung on the hillsides. It was mainly women who set out their wares. They brought it to market in woven string bags called *bilum bags* which they supported on their back and across the brow of their heads as they made their precarious way down through the hill paths.

The produce was all freshly picked that morning and laid out beautifully on the tables or on top of large banana tree leaves on the ground. Bunches of bananas, pineapples, small yellow coloured oranges, lemons, mangos, sweet potatoes (kau kau), avocados and tomatoes were all on sale. I went there with my mum who picked her way through the sellers offering fruit and vegetables at incredibly low prices. Like any market, the idea was to bargain and ask for *"first price"* then *" best price"* but I'm fairly sure mum never drove a hard bargain, payment was always met with broad smiles and thank you from the sellers.

Something which you first notice about the appearance of many of the natives is a deep ochre red colouration around their lips and mouths. This results from the chewing of a particular kind of beetle. It was always very common on market days and at the market itself, probably because the beetles were sold or exchanged there. I don't remember our mum ever making an offer to buy beetles though, first price, best price or any price.

Our mum seemed to have a slightly different teaching contract to our Dad. For some reason her pay arrived in cash every few weeks when the plane landed and it was picked up from the safe at the airstrip building. Mum was in a habit of bringing her pay home in an envelope, walking through from the kitchen and launching all the cash into the air in the living room. We all scrambled to gather up all the cash and held onto it for a wee while. Mum would then say *"Right, let's have all the cash back now please"* and she'd count it all up to see none was missing!

We visited some nearby villages in the first months in Kerowagi but there weren't many of any great size. People in the highlands still lived spread out as much as possible, they'd had no reason to build larger settlements until motorised transport arrived. One nearby place we'd heard about was the village of Kup (pronounced *"Koop"*). We drove down to the Koronigl bridge and turned right, then around ten miles westwards along the Highlands Highway in the direction of Mount Hagen. We then turned off the highway along a rough road for a few miles to the village of Kup. The village was beautifully laid out and well worth the trip. The houses were all built in bamboo pit-pit and grassed roofs but possibly the best examples in the western highlands at the time. The locals had decided there would be none of the new style buildings in the village of Kup and is seemed a great decision, like a conservation village where people realised the beauty of what they built from their surroundings.

Meeting Houses in the village of Kup

The Crate - (part 2)
As the months went by, we were getting accustomed to the people, the town, the highlands and our new way of life. On school days we made the trip to and from Kundiawa Primary "A" School where we were educated along the lines of the Australian education system along with around thirty other ex-patriot children. Their parents had ventured into Chimbu district to work in teaching, admin, retail and missionary work or for the ongoing construction of the Highlands Highway. To try to educate us alongside the native children would never have been practical as the main priority in the local primary schools was to teach native children pigeon English (tok pisin) rather than their local dialect then move on to learn English. Hence our parents drove the arduous 17 mile journey over bumpy stone roads to drop us at Kundiawa primary on all school days and came back to collect us after school.

All the while, in our remote new world, we awaited the arrival of the crate. The crate, which promised much of what was missing from our old life in the developed world. It seemed to take an eternity to arrive. Maybe it did go all the way to Manus Island then get redirected back across the Bismark Sea and into the highlands? Quite possibly, that would explain the months it took to reach us. When the crate finally arrived it was quite an anti-climax. Maybe we should have realised, our parents maybe already did, but very few of the items we'd packed so thoughtfully before leaving were of any real use in Kerowagi. My Triang 70 bicycle with its fashionable small wheel concept rattled up and down on the stony roads of the school compound to the point that it was much easier just to walk or run. My leather football had gone flat and I hadn't packed an adaptor to inflate it. Toys and trucks lacked any smooth outdoor surface to run on and besides, we'd now outgrown most of them.

So much for the crate! Even the vacuum cleaner was of no real use as the wooden floors were swept each day by a house boy who came to work for us and I think we may have given him most of the blankets. There was one thing in that crate however which was roundly appreciated by all the family and people who came to visit our home, the record player. The record player and the dozen or so vinyl records packed with it brought the music of the New Seekers, Nana Mouskouri, Peter Paul & Mary and even some Scottish country dance music to the highlands of Papua New Guinea. The record player was put on a table just outside our bedrooms and we loved listening to it in the evenings and falling asleep to the music. It filled our house with music and some memories of our life at home in Scotland.

*"Remember how we wiled away the hours,
Thinking of the great things we would do,
Those were the days my friend,
We thought they'd never end,
We'd sing and dance, forever and a day....."*

*"Tell me my dove,
Where can I find the Olive tree
Is it there above the clouds,
Or beyond the stormy sky...."*

Electrical power was supplied by a generator located near the hospital. It purred away in the distance in a way that you didnt notice the sound until it fell silent around nine p.m. at night. A few seconds after we heard it stop, the lights would all go out. If a record was playing the music would slow down as the turntable then ground to a hault with the needle still lying on the record. Our parents would then light up the kerosine lamp to give some light for the rest of the evening.

As to any other items in the crate, the game of monopoly deserves a mention, it was useful occasionally during the weeks of the rainy season. The rest was of little use. Most things which seem important in a family home in Scotland had no practical use in the Western Highlands of PNG. New and interesting things all happened outdoors, dad had built a barbecue and a mini golf course in our garden. The adults would all visit their colleagues houses for drinks and I remember their conversations at our first barbecue in the garden, *"The standard of living is great here"* they were saying, as they dropped the ice into their martinis. Food and other supplies were not expensive, probably because goods also had to be affordable to the native people when possible. It was common for us to cook fillet steaks and T-bone steaks on the barbecue and our dad left us to cook them as he chatted and drank his SP beer. Everything we needed came from either Heagney's store, Steamships Trading in Kundiawa or fresh from the local market.

Pipty & Mac

We had two pets in our home in Kerowagi and I can't say who came first as they came almost at the same time. We named our car "Pipty" which was actually pigeon English for fifty. We got her in Kundiawa and when people were offering kittens at that time you had to pay at least fifty cents for them. The woman who sold us Pipty explained that this was to set a price higher than the native people were prepared to pay as they were likely to raise the cat to a point where they would then eat it. The price tag was enough to put them off buying the cat as fifty cents would buy them more nutrition elsewhere.

We acquired our dog Mac as a tiny puppy in Kerowagi itself from some people who lived in a house on the road up towards the club. We went to look at the litter and Dad reckoned Mac seemed to come towards us so he was the chosen one. Mac and Pipty then grew up together and they spent the first few months of their lives with Mac chasing Pipty everywhere and never quite catching her. As we came down the path after school some days a small black ball of fluff would flash across the steps in front of you and less than a second later a light brown and white one wold come tearing after her. As it turned out they became incredibly good friends. Even when they were fully grown, Pipty would lie between Mac's front and back paws as he slept and when she was finished licking and cleaning herself she would start to clean Mac!

Pipty was a character and really could look after herself, maybe as a result of growing up with Mac. She was an outright expert thief. Anything which was left on plates was fair game the way she saw it but also anything laid out ready to cook. We devised ways of trying to keep stuff well out of her way but over time she still found ways to steal it. On more than one occasion she managed to steal fillet steaks and by the time we caught her it was usually too late to rescue them.

Mac turned into a beautiful big dog. You couldn't really buy dog food at Mr Heagney's store but you could buy tinned fish (*"tin-pis"*) and we also kept large sacks of rice. As it happens, tin-pis and boiled rice was a favourite meal of the local people. I was a good addition to their diet but it was also the easiest way to feed Mac and he really thrived on it. He was the fittest and best looking dog for miles around as you can imagine. This also meant he was very active on the mating scene as a young fellow. We used to chuckle as time went on as you passed people with litters of dogs in Kerowagi and they all looked like Mac!

Mac was also important as a guard dog and he was a very good one. The only problem was that he could clearly tell white skinned people from dark skinned people. He had figured out that all the white people who came to visit were our friends but he'd bark at the native people or any of our friends who were black. It was an unfortunate thing at times and actually quite difficult to train him out of. He used to accompany Rog and I on our adventures down at the Tem Creek. We quickly learned that if we were on the wrong side of the creek, local native children could be very hostile to us. At first we didn't realise it was instilled in them that anyone on their land wasn't welcome unless invited. On one day we thought some of the native boys were trying to start a chasing game with us but pretty soon some punches were landing from a group gathering around us. These were boys of our age, nine or ten years old, some younger. It was then that Mac sprang into action. He had them all warded off from us in no time and as we hurried back across the creek he still had them well at a distance.

On another occasion, we were down by the creek playing with Charlie and Eddie Ariston and we came across a large adder on the narrow path down to the water. It was coiled up in the strike position it had taken up as we approached and Mac scurried right up to it and started barking wildly. He also took up a pounce position himself with his paws stretched out in front, just short of the snake. We were all screaming at him and calling him off and thankfully after pouncing back and forwards a couple of times he got the message and ran back to us. We were very relieved to find he was unharmed and the snake hadn't managed to bite him.

Mac also used to love going to the club with us at weekends. He'd realise quite quickly where we were going as we assembled with our swimming and tennis gear and then follow us out to the car. As we backed onto the roadway to move off, he'd be on the road in front of us and start running ahead of the car. He knew the way to the club which was about a mile and a half away and it was impossible to overtake him. His tail swished from side to side and he cast glances over his shoulder as he ran on ahead to make sure we were still there behind him. When we reached the club he'd be panting and take a drink of water from the pool. As soon as any one of us jumped in he was straight in after us, in fact he may have jumped in before us at times but he loved going to the club even more than we did.

CHAPTER 5 - THE NATIVES OF CHIMBU

The natives living at 6000 feet high up in the Chimbu District were a truly startling race of people. They lived mainly a subsistence living back in 1973 but seemed universally happy most of the time. They could be quite edgy and a little uncomfortable with the sudden arrival and influence of western culture but their over-riding nature was friendly and welcoming. In the early 1970's they were trying to strike a balance between being in awe at western culture whilst trying to deal with the influxes it brought their way. You could sense the change going on almost every day, the mixture of joy and excitement at the arrival of cars, trucks and aeroplanes, but a sense of puzzlement about what it all meant. Their culture was still very much tribal with a large number of tribes (hundreds) occupying Chimbu District.

Chimbu was the main emerging district in the Western Highlands of PNG during our time there. The highlands highway was under major construction and had opened up the region from obscurity. Further west lay the Mount Hagen region and then deeper rain forest. To the north lay the massive Bismark Mountain range. It was all a new and sometimes confusing time for the natives of Chimbu back then though. They had a reputation for a lot of waring among the tribes and much of it was over land which was becoming highly prized for plantation, especially coffee plantation. Hence one of the most striking tribal ceremonies you could witness, a tradition called "payback". At times when tribes ran out of appetite for ongoing war, peace settlements were sometimes struck. Once agreed, this made for a huge ceremonial display of recompense from one tribe to the other. We witnessed one major pay back during a lull in the war between the Siku and Genna tribes, the two major rival tribes in Chimbu at the time. Payback meant the erecting of massive bamboo display banners, often with thousands of dollar bills mounted on them. The tribes then marched, danced and sang their way to their rival's territory to hand over the payback.

The photograph above is contained in an album of black and white photos given to our parents by their colleague Mr John Blacksland and the caption in the album says the Sikus are bringing $3,500 to the Genna tribe after making a temporary peace in in 1974. The death count amounted to single figures as far as we knew but the loss of only one or two lives more in the Genna tribe gave rise to this payback. We all witnessed the payback and felt the tension in the air that day. John Blacksland has ventured close to the roadway to take this photo or maybe he had a long-range lens. You wouldn't want to get in the way of these guys for very long, as you can imagine. It was a peace offering but also a show of strength and a warning. For the tribes to arrive at this sort of consensus was very impressive but it didn't always mean the fighting was at an end.

Another exchange which often featured in Payback was an allocation of pigs. Pigs were extremely important in Chimbu culture and elsewhere in PNG. Pigs were considered a sacred animal in the Western Highlands and a unit of exchange in addition to the Australian dollar currency. Tribes people looked after them in the same way they looked after their children. We were warned in our early days there that it you were to run over a pig on the road, keep driving, don't stop to apologise or you might be lucky to escape with your life. On visits to the market, native women could be seen cuddling their baby pigs close in, like an infant child and on one early visit to the market I first witnesses a native woman suckling a baby pig to her breast.

In the highlands the natives still wore predominantly grass skirts but as time went on, shorts and shirts were becoming more common on visits to the towns and villages. Each tribe had their own very distinctive ceremonial dress though and went to incredible lengths on major occasions. Tribal dress included bones inserted through the nose and ears, and also fantastic head dresses which included the much coveted plumage of the birds of paradise resident in and around the rain forests. There were ceremonial occasions locally and tribes often travelled hundreds of miles to take part in larger show gatherings, the Goroka and

Mount Hagen Shows.

Our closest contact to a local person came in the form of Ilap, our house boy. It seems a little shameful on reflection having a house boy but he and others had been very interested in the job. On the first or second day of waking up in our new home, a few well presented young guys arrived on the doorstep of our house with reference papers asking for the job of house boy. His job was to help cook, clean and maintain the house. After some consultation with other staff at the school, Ilap was taken on as the houseboy. He was a very pleasant guy and the source of much local knowledge and amusement. He helped us learn the local language which was called *"Tok Pisin"* (talk pidgin). Like most local people, Ilap spoke his local dialect and also Tok Pisin which helped provide a common dialect. There were many different dialects, hundreds of then in the highlands and all over PNG. We learned from Ilap as he learned more English from us. *"Mi-yu kookim dispela sikin"*... let's cook this chicken. We could all tok pisin pretty well as time went on. I can still remember some but wouldn't be able to hold down a conversation like we did back then.

Much was expected of Ilap, including some baking. He didnt bake bread, we were able to buy bread in the form of "tank loaves", so named because of their simlar corrugated shape to the large water storage tanks all around. He did bake cakes though using cake mixes bought from Steamships Trading Company. For some reason these cakes rose at the sides but barely at all in the middle. Ilap made up for this by speading the icing level across the cake! He would lay these cakes down on the table and say simply "Cek". Everyone smiled at the prospect and the off chance that one day the cake would have risen in the middle but it never did. As kids we actually hoped not, we loved Ilap's icing packed cakes! Ilap also helped with lots of local knowlege in the garden. It was Ilap who showed us how to keep the tops cut from pineapples in some water for a while then plant them. He who showed us how to grow the peanuts. When he decided they were ready, we dug them up, shelled them out and he put them on a tray with some salt and roasted them in the oven. They tasted better than anything you'd ever buy in a packet, fresh peanuts straight from the garden, salted and roasted by Ilap!

The natives were impressive in the way they lived their lives on little resource and in harmony with their surroundings. A resilient, combative but fascinating nation of people. In the evenings when we first arrived in Kerowagi we became aware of a type of singing from down in the Tem Creek where the land dropped away sharply to the west of our house. The sound was like a rambling chorus echoing off down the valley. As we came to realise, this was how communication passed all over the highlands of Papua New Guinea. We lived right on one of the arteries where news was hollered out in the quiet of the evening, when the sound seemed to travel best. *"Ooola moola boola woola bayo, bondo moolo boola holloa wayo"* that's how it sounded, but like a song which dropped in pitch right at the end of each message then it drifted off down the valley, almost as if to say "over and out. pass it on". My brother and sister and I learned to mimic the sound as we lay in our beds, we still can to this day. *"Walla boola goola monna donna bayo, balla wolla hayo...!"*

These bush telegraphs apparently travelled for miles and miles through the valleys and between the mountains, where the acoustics were tried and proven. Men and women stood at defined distances along the valleys and sang out these choruses until all the day's news was spread in one direction and then all the way back. Who knows we may even have been part of the news some nights. *"New white family in last house at top end of the school compound, still no house boy appointed... Oola boola woola bayo!.... White people have stopped the stream again, I had a bath in their pool this morning before sunrise" .... Boonda moono woolo bollo.... Great, but move that metal thing and get the stream back on please! ..... Did you get any more beer from their meeting house? .....Tomorrow! .....balla wolla hayo!"* We fell asleep to the distant hollering most evenings with news travelling far and wide as it had done for centuries gone by.

The Bogo Road

Beyond the north end of the airstrip and round the east side of Mum's mountain lay the Bogo Road. The Bogo road, spoken about in almost mythical terms by our parents' circle of friends at school, by Ilap and other people in and around Kerowagi. It led up the Korunigl valley as it carved its way into the Bismark Mountain range to the north. The prospect of going there was exciting, the Bogo road wasn't really considered part of the approved road network. The trip had been well planned, it needed to be, given the hazards of the road and the absence of anything other than tribal law and lifestyle once five or ten miles up the cavernous valley. For a while it looked like my sister brother and I wouldn't be on the trip but the presence of Charlie Ariston, Bill Graham the Kiap (and his shotgun) along with our dad seemed to swing the decision in our favour. The Public Works Department trucks had also been secured on loan for the trip as no ordinary car or vehicle could tackle the road to Bogo.

We left early in the morning in our shorts, t-shirts and flip-flop shoes like any other day but with picnics packed and excitement in the air. Charlie and Bill drove PWD truck in front while our dad and John Pickles drove the other. There were seven or eight people in each truck with three sitting up front and the rest in the open back holding onto the railings. We drove north past the top end of the village, rounded the north end of the airstrip, down to the Koronigl river then started off up the valley on road leading to bogo village . This same road was used by anyone wishing to travel on to Mount Wilhelm the highest mountain in Papau new Guinea.

As with every early morning in Chimbu District, mist and clouds hung in the valley in every hollow, in the forests and on the hillsides. The Bogo road was no more than a two wheel track which followed the west side of the river as it wound its way up the valley. It was the dry season but still the moisture dripped from the trees into the Koronigl river torrent as it rumbled away down the steep valley below. (To have tried to tackle the Bobo road in the rainy season would have been madness!) We held tight to the rails as the trucks lurched forward into every gulley and the gears crashed as they climbed the steep rises.

On we drove, with our drivers not really accustomed to the vehicles, even less to the terrain. Occasionally, native tribes people could be seen high to our left staring at us from their bamboo homesteads and making their way down to the roadside as we approached. They often shouted to us as we passed, in their form of greeting, "ayeee, ayeee" either as a friendly greeting or in surprise at seeing our convoy making its way into their territory. To our right, the sound of the river grew louder as we ran closer to it, then quieter as we veered away a little, but never far. From time to time makeshift bridges appeared across the ravine. These bridges all looked ingenious and all the while precarious crossings, where fallen trees had been secured high above narrow gorges where the river flowed fastest. The wet surfaces were criss-crossed with vines to provide footholds for the men women and children who crept across these bridges, like tight rope walkers with their toes gripping the vines.

The day grew warmer quickly as the sun rose above the mountains and as ever the cool morning mists gave way to the humidity as we stopped for drinks. Through the tropical pine trees, we could see the mountains rising sharply above the valley on all sides. Narrow paths here and there made their way up from the river to small clusters of bamboo huts clinging to the hillsides next to the small but ever present terraced fields carved onto the adjacent slopes.

We loaded back into our trucks and pressed on the roller coaster ride, up towards the village of Bogo. We didn't stop for long, you never did when out in the "bush" or the "outback", as the Aussies would say. There was one last climb as I remember it, the river seemed to be calming a little then the truck veered over a summit, as we looked down on Bogo. The village lay in a lush open clearing in the valley, a cluster of bamboo huts as always and some larger huts recognisable as meeting places and the head man's house. Villagers gradually appeared from all around to greet us and also to stare at our expedition in curiosity. The younger children all giggled and looked at us in amazement.

Some men and women got together in a confab and I think the adults in our group spoke to them including our Kiap Bill Graham who helped put the people at ease. Bill seemed to have a real knack when dealing with local people, he had a quietly assured Irish accent and a well looked after shotgun near at hand. Most of the amazement was at us and our appearance, even despite the sun tans many of us had acquired. Many of these villagers had rarely, if ever seen white people. We didn't stay long but we stayed long enough to share a drink and what conversation was possible with the villagers. Just before we left, some children and one girl in particular approached the truck and looked right into the driver's seats. Someone who was sitting up front then turned on the radio and the young girl stepped back in amazement. Some other people came forward to listen to the voices from the dash board and all jumped back, in a mixture of fear and astonishment. Ghosts and spirits played a huge part in New Guinean folklore and I'm sure that's how they interpreted the voices from the radio.

It was time to leave, with one look back over the brow of the hill to the village of Bogo, the most untouched place we visited in all our time in PNG and some villagers we'd never forget. Likewise, they'd remember our visit and probably take note and ponder on who'd come next and how the outside world would creep into their lives over time. Some of the villagers followed our trucks for a while then gave up as we bumped and slid our way back down their valley, ghosts and spirits in our wake.

The Goroka and Mount Hagen Shows

At some point fairly early in our first year in PNG, our parents took possession of our new car, a light green Toyota Carina. It wasn't the most suitable vehicle in many ways but with a few modifications, it soon went into action. Larger truck size tyres were fitted to the wheels in preparation for the rough roads and something called a sump guard to protect the engine from the bumping, crunching and flying rocks it could expect to endure. After a good amount of trial and testing on the daily 17 mile school run to Kundiawa the trusty car was set for a trip back through the mountains to Goroka. Our destination was the Goroka Show, one of the largest get-togethers taking place in the highlands of Papua New Guinea in 1973 and a growing attraction.

We drove down from Kerowagi to the Koronigl bridge then south on the highway to Kundiawa. The trip was now familiar to us and was a mixture of the old road and makeshift tracks to and from the newly built sections of the Highway. At the time it took us around 40 minutes to drive the 17 miles to our school in Kundiawa. From Kundiawa itself we continued east, down from the plateau of the town to the bridge over the Chimbu river which lay directly south of the town, in the valley beneath Kundiawa airstrip. We had friends from school, the Collins family who lived there in a ranch type house on their coffee plantation but within a few minutes of crossing the bridge we were in completely new territory.

The road back to Goroka was arduous over the mountains and across a summit at the Daulo Pass. Like the highway being built to the west, the road was all stone surfaced and a mixture of old and newer sections. In many places it descended to no more than a muddy track. The scenery was as breath taking as ever. In places the road was surrounded by vegetation but it could suddenly open out to reveal the hills and valleys with the clouds clinging to the hillsides. The mist and clouds rose quickly in the late morning as we made our way across the mountains toward Mount Elimbari. The imposing shape of mount Elimbari could be seen from all over the district of Chimbu. We saw it in the distance every morning on our trip to school but now we made our way slowly and surely towards it. There was no other mountain shaped quite like in either. It had an asymmetrical craggy appearance. It stuck out starkly from the surrounding landscape, mountainous as it was. As a boy it seemed to me it might be a launch pad for rockets.

Mount Elimbari

We passed through village after village, most of them no more than a collection of pit-pit huts adjacent to the road. The natives of these villages all stopped to watch us pass. We'd grown used to bein curiously now, some waved and some sang out greetings. Our car was an unusual vehicle to be making this journey, most were much heavier trucks. In places the people sold fruit and vegetables at the side of the road. Occasionally we'd stop and buy a pineapple or tomatoes to add to our picnic and drinks stops. There was rarely any hostility encountered on the roads but we were aware of the dangers. In general, advice was not to stop in any of these villages at least not for any length of time. We stopped in quieter areas for lunch and frequent drinks stops as the day grew warmer and the journey grew wearier.

At the larger rivers, heavy wooden bridges had been built but for all the smaller streams and rivers, we drove across fords. Some of the fords were a real challenge for our car and exciting for us children in the back seat, but didnt seem just as much fun for our mother sitting up front. We made it through all these fords but truthfully it's hard to believe we were never stuck mid stream. When we pulled up and looked at some of them we really had our doubts, especially at the biggest one. It was the one notorious ford on the road to Goroka at which vehicles often foundered. One thing we could be grateful for, it wasn't the rainy season. Our dad actually seemed to enjoy the fords, which helped us all to do the same. The plan was just to pick a route then put the foot down and drive, without slowing down and plough on at all costs.

The car bumped crunched and at times almost swam its way over. Despite the plan to drive straight, the car seemed to point one way then the other as the rear of the car swung in opposite directions. If we seemed to slow or come against larger rocks, dad accelerated on, and over we went. It was exhilarating and often a big relief to make it over and met with a great family cheer!

At last in the late afternoon after climbing for many long hours into the mountains, we arrived at Daulo Summit. There was a large washed out sign post to mark the spot and we stopped to take photographs and briefly take in the views. We looked down into the valley and could already see Goroka in the distance. The road carved great red scores into the side of the mountain on the north side of the valley as it descended from the summit. This part of the road was far better constructed and the journey seemed to pass much more quickly into Goroka where we arrived in the evening. We arrived back at the Minagere motel where we'd stayed many months ago on our initial trip north from Port Moresby.

A view from near Daulo Pass towards Goroka

There were two reasons for travelling back to Goroka as far as I recall. The first was to visit the Goroka show, the other was that we were also travelling on to the town of Lae, on the North coast of PNG for a week's holiday. That night in the Minagere Motel foyer, our Dad pointed out a bill hoarding with an advert for a feature at the Goroka show the next day. It was advertising *"Rod Flewellen"* the bird man! There were many things we'd heard about at the Goroka show: the tribal displays, tribes people from Papua in the south, from the Sepic River in the far north, the famous mud-men. Rod Flewellen was unexpected and had additional billing around the town suggesting Rod was a winged man and was going to fly into the show. No amount of questioning gave us any more insight, apart from our Dad saying he was probably Welsh. *"You'll just have to wait and see kids!"*

One thing about the proud tribal people of Papua New Guinea, they loved nothing more than a ceremonial gathering, the bigger the better. So much so that all differences, waring and any other quarrels were set aside for such events. Events like the Goroka show were eagerly awaited and tribes people travelled there from hundreds of miles across the highlands and all the way from Papua in the south. Each tribe had their own very unique and fabulous appearance when they wore their own interpretaions of what they called "National Dress". Head dresses were adorned with the feathers of the birds of paradise which inhabited the forests. Bodies and faces were painted with the pigments found local to the tribes and the grass skirts or "arse grass" worn for these occasions were greener, fresher and more elaborate than those worn day to day. Loud dances and tribal chants broke out from time to time with each tribe reacting to the other and there was a high police presence at these shows, just in case any old or recent vendettas should raise their heads.

As if to ease some of the tension in the air, eyes turned to the skies as the show drew near to a close. High up in the sky was a small white and green spec with a bright smoke trail following behind it. Was it a bird, was it a plane? No, it was Rod Flewellen, the bird man! People began to cheer with excitement as he swirled gradually down towards the show ground. People shuffled, chanted and laughed in nervous excitement. As Rod appeared closer we could see the large green "SP" letters emblazened on the wings of his hang glider advertising the South Pacific beer company. It was the first time we'd encountered hang gliding and going by their reaction, the first time for the tribes at the Goroka show. Shortly afterwards as he arrived almost at ground level, Rod somehow flew back up a little then practically crashed to the ground.

Men in grass shirts rushed towards him to check all was well and some policemen followed. Rod seemed absolutely fine and his broad smile and hugs and waves for all were testament to his wellbeing. The people of Papua New Guinea were in awe at the many aircraft appearing in their skies in those times and Rod Flewellen "the bird man", was no exception. The South Pacific beer company could also be very well pleased with him, it was a job well done. You could only hope there were enough crates of South Pacific beer in Goroka that evening for everyone to raise a glass to Rod!

Tribesmen at the Goroka Show

We also drove north to the Mount Hagen show once the Highland Highway had improved in our second year in PNG. This was an even larger tribal gathering with huge contingents able to travel there from the Bayer river, Sepic river and other large river valleys which stretched well into the west, (the wild west!) the north and over the border into West Irian. At the height of the festivities, each tribe performed their tribal war dance, complete with their best spears and weapons. These displays were spectacular. Police forces were starting to build up in all the main towns of PNG at the time and a strong presence was again present at the Hagen show. The main purpose of these war dances was ostensibly tribal gathering and display but you could feel the real tension in the air at the height of the show. There was no doubting that another purpose of these tribes making the journey to the Goroka show was for a show of strength year on year and a loud warning to other tribes. What a spectacle!

Mass tribal gathering at the Hagen Show

At the end of this book there's a brief review of some stamps I collected as a boy during this time in PNG in 1973/74. One set of stamps shows the birds of paradise of PNG, the feathers and plumages of which adorn the head dresses reserved for these gatherings. I express my sincere hopes that all the species shown on the stamps are still in existance. The thoughts are maybe best be expressed in a poem I then wrote as I was finishing this book and I include it now, as a break in the narrative rather than leave it to the end.

The Kumul

High in his hidden nest in the sky
Under the twinkling array
Sleeps the handsome kumul
With his colours supressed in the grey
The quiet of the forest gives comfort and rest
Till he wakes to the sounds of the day

Sunrise comes gently to the canopy heights
As his newfound partner sings
His beautiful colours awakened and bright
The young kumul shakes dew from his wings
But sought by the hunter with his arrows and bow
Who sleeps in the shadows below

The kumul's new quarry approaches

WALTER LINTON

As she flies to her mate in the trees
And there in the braches she swoons and she sways
As he flutters and jumps in the breeze
He puffs out his plumage and sings out his song
His instinctive fantastic display
She's entranced by his wonderful colours
Enflamed by the heat of the day
Now seen by the hunter, with his arrows and bow
As he hides in the shadows below

Their courtship approaches its climax
As they tumble and leap in romance
"Paradisaea Decora"
Two kumuls in rapturous dance
But the keen young hunter is skilful
As he lines up his arrows and bow
For he wants these same plumes for a head-dress
He'll wear at the Mount Hagen show

These plumages never so brightly displayed
As only his lady could know
She could see no sensible reason
For why he'd abandon his show
She had lost her young bloke at the dancing
And it troubled her heart to the core
Was be back in his nest taking refuge?
Or did he fall to the rainforest floor?

We pray that the eager young hunter
Some day and before it's too late
That he'll spare the wonderful kumul
And leave him to dance with his mate
For the hunter too can dance and sing
With the girls at the Mount Hagen show
Soon he'll find himself a young lover
And put down his arrows and bow.

CHAPTER 6 - HOLIDAYS

The road trip to Lae

From Goroka we embarked once again on the ongoing trip to Lae, we may have stayed another day at the Minagere to relax and recover from the Goroka show. The road to Lae was better, wider and a little faster going. There was also a little more traffic on the road compared to our journey over Daulo. The ongoing journey required two more days travelling. On the first day the journey was mountainous all day long and as usual it got warmer as we went, with almost every coner giving way to a new vista with high and impressive mountains all around. We climbed steep inclines and the road traversed the valleys and hillsides as we made our way to our mid-way destination where we arrived in the late afternoon in time for dinner. The town of Kainantu had a few well spread out houses, some shops on the main road and a filling station. We arrived at a basic motel for travellers, Kainantu had a real staging post feel to it. Nonetheless, it felt good to reach the comfort of the motel after the long and arduous ascent from Goroka.

The next day after a good rest and breakfast at the motel, we filled the car full of petrol and set off for the town of Lae on the North coast. There was much anticipation that morning as we approached the most memorable feature of the journey to Lae. It lay a few hours ahead in the form of the Kassam Pass. It didn't disappoint that's for sure, an amazing place. As we got closer to the pass itself, we could feel the air getting rapidly warmer. The view to the north was out across the wide and endless Margam valley, what a sight! After approaching through mountainous roads, everything opened out across the precipice, the mountains fell sharply away, thousands of feet towards the valley below. When we had stopped the car at the view point, we then caught site of the road down from the pass to the valley and we'd never seen a road like it. It snaked out one way then back the other, down the steep drop into the valley. *"My god"* mum was saying, *"we're going to drive down that road!"* The bends at each corner were sharp hairpin turns, every one without exception and all the way to the valley floor. There were far fewer trees and greenery on the hillsides now and felt the warm breeze blowing steadily as we stepped out of the car for refeshment and yet more drinks.

View from the Kassam Pass as the road descends into the Margam Valley

Most travellers stopped for a little while at the Kassam pass, to rest, take in the view of the vast Margam valley and prepare for the ongoing journey. Soon we could delay no longer and drove off down the snaking road. Each corner was taken with great care as we dropped and there were signs in several places of the very large mud slides which often left the road impassable. As we descended we could blow out the pressure in our ears just as we'd learned to do in aeroplanes. On reaching the valley floor, the road then stretched out straight into the distance. The cool of the mountains was now completely gone and the road just stretched on and on along the wide valley floor. Stones kicked up from the road surface and rattled and bashed constantly against the underside of the car as we travelled at higher speed. Our mum also took turns driving a little more slowly than dad but they both had to slow down often when the noise of the battering stones grew too loud on the underside of the car. Occasionally we could feel larger stones smacking right under our feet. The road shimmered ahead in the heat haze and merged into a boiling blur where it disappeared at the vanishing point. The rest of the journey grew long and tedious with little to see at the roadsides. Some way along the valley a ridge of mountains appeared to the west side of the highway called the Saw Tooth mountains. The ridge rose high above the valley and was well named with jagged tooth like peaks running regularly along the skyline.

We drove on with the windows wide open on what was now a baking hot day. Those with window seats put their ams outside regularly to try to cool off. We all became a little irritable until an abrupt and unexpected sensation as we arrived five or ten miles from Lae. The noise of the stones smacking against the underside of the car suddenly died away to be replaced by a gentle high pitched hum of our tyres against the road. The surface had changed from stones to tarmac! It was the most pleasant sensation as everyone in the car agreed. Wow! tarmac, we've arrived in the outskirts of Lae.

We finally drove into the hotel car park, opened all the car doors and spilled out into the cooler air of the evening. The name of this hotel has escaped me for some years now, it was something like the Colonies or the Plantations Hotel. It took the form of a central bar and restaurant area with rows of chalets on small stilts at regular intervals along the walk-way past the swimming pool. Just after we arrived we all went to the bar and our parents ordered drinks. They drank things like beer, shandies, martinis and cinzanos in PNG, who could blame them. It was at that bar I asked for a coca cola which was easily the best one I've ever experienced. It was handed from the bar in an ice cold bottle with the top flipped off the much awaited and very refreshing drink. Only my second visit to a hotel bar since the Port Moresby *monsters* incident and that coca cola was just terrific. Every time I enjoy an ice cold coca cola on a hot day, it still takes me back to that one in the hotel bar in Lae.

Arrival at the hotel in Lae.

In the evenings after dinner it always felt good to walk out into the cool breeze. At the entrance to the bar & restaurant there was an area where local people laid out their wares for sale to the hotel residents. These were beautifully crafted items, very nicely laid out on the tiled floor and we rarely walked past them without taking a good look. Our parents bought carvings mostly of masks, bowls and fishes but also a bead curtain for our kitchen. Our sister Janet could browse there forever, she bought some really distinctive shell necklaces and bangles. All of these things eventually came home with us to Scotland, the masks are still hanging on the walls of our family home forty five years on and counting.

We had a terrific time in Lae. We were able to swim again for days and days on end like back in Port Moresby. There were some Australian kids at the hotel who were intent on teaching us how to dive in dangerously. *Bloody bute! Bomb the Pommies!* Dive in front ways, dive in back ways, splash bombs, and back flip. The splash bomb was one we already knew!

We ventured into the main town of Lae on more than one occasion for walks along the sea front and for shopping as far as I remember. We watched the locals going out fishing from the shoreline in their hollowd out canoes. We collected all sorts of large and unusual shaped shells completely different from those back home in Scotland.

The streets were wide streets with tarmac roads which was a real pleasure each time we encountered them in PNG. There were rows of one level shops along the main street and most of them run by Chinese traders. We took the chance to shop for clothes which were more befitting to life in PNG and bought new flip flops and swimming costumes.

One shop we visited was a camera and watch shop where my brother and I went with our dad while our mum and Janet were shopping elsewhere. He'd already bought a camera on the flight from UK when we stopped at Singapore but on this occasion dad was on the lookout for a good watch, a "Seiko" watch in particular.

The shop owner was a Chinese guy and he had a lot of Seiko watches to show dad and a lot to say about them. The watch which dad seemed to like the most was being sold as an unbreakable watch. In a startling move, the salesman quite deliberately dropped the watch straight onto the floor. He then retrieved the watch and laid it back on the counter to show it was unmarked and still keeping perfect time. Dad was pretty impressed and laughing away with the guy, he turned to my brother and me smiling and said *"Did you see that lads?"* He said to the guy *"OK, I'll buy this watch"* but he quickly followed this with *"Can I have one which is still in its' box please?"* My brother Roger still has possession of that Seiko watch. He renovated it around forty years on from our trip and added a stylish new strap. I'll remind him of our visit to the shop in Lae and maybe he'll treasure the unbreakable Seiko all the more.

The Trip to Madang
We made at least two main holiday trips each year during our stay in Papua New Guinea each year to both Lae and Madang on the North coast of PNG, with a trip to Sydney Australia at the end of our first year. Because our dad had the overseas allowance paid to him and our mum had also found a teaching job straight away with the PNG government, it seemed we could afford to go almost anywhere and we did, and to all the best places. Whilst we tackled

the epic car trip to Lae in our Toyota Carina car, Madang lay further north so our parents chartered a flight for us. Yes, an exclusive family flight which took off from Kuniawa airstrip and flew up directly over the Bismark Mountain range from Kundiawa to Madang. Flying north from Kundiawa meant tearing down the short airstrip and off the end as the Chimbu river valley lay below us then banking steep left, high into the mountains. We made these charter flights in six or ten seat Cessna aircraft. Looking back on the flights in these aircraft over the Bismark mountains they seemed daring and genuinely mad, even at the time. Once we'd made the initial trip all the way into the highlands, in smaller and smaller planes though, we eventually though nothing of it.

The Cessna our parents chartered for our trip to Madang

The Cessna flew gradually upwards through one valley after another, close to the mountain sides and hopping over the passes. Finally, we reached the highest point in the flight as we flew through an aerial pass in the mountains called the Bismark Gap. I remember dad telling us the highest mountain in PNG, Mount Wilhelm was around 15,000 feet high. We must have been well over 10,000 feet up to get through the Bismark Gap and as always, there were times when we were no more than thirty of forty feet from the mountainsides. We saw every village, river and waterfall as we passed by and now and then, just as things were feeling steady, we flew blind through the low lying banks of clouds which hung in the valleys. These memoirs may serve to help remind our mum of these exciting Cessna flights, whether she'll want to be reminded I'm not certain!

Views from the Cessna on route to Madang

As we appoached Madang we could see miles and miles of

coconut and banana plantations surrounding the town in all directions. We got closer and closer to the tops of the plam trees before landing in the small airport in Madang. To the east of the town in a small bay lay the Smugglers Inn, where we went to stay for a week. Madang was a wonderfully scenic town, a resort you would maybe say, as a resorts might be classed in 1973, on the beautiful north coast of PNG. To the west end of the town at the sea front there was large tower which was called the Coastguards Monument, commemorating people who'd flown and fought in the second world war in the South Pacific. All around the town and along the sea front there were floral bushes and our mum would comment on them as we passed. "Look at these beautiful hibiscus bushes" and "Aren't these wonderful frangipani bushes". I remember them being covered in large, mostly red, white and pink flowers.

Reception at the Smugglers Inn

We turned off the coast road into a small lane which led

to the Smugglers Inn. Floral bushes grew up the walls all around the archway which led to the reception. In our memories the "Smugglers" remains probably the best place we've holidayed in our lifetime, close to what people might picture as paradise. It was the height of luxury for the 1970s in PNG. In the main building behind reception was the air conditioned bar and restaurant which then led out to a broad terrace bounded by a small sea wall. We often sat on the wall as the waves of the South Pacific Ocean broke on the rocks just below. On some evenings the chefs cooked open air barbecues on the terrace, one of which was a Chinese barbecue during our stay. Our first introduction to Chinese cooking, for us children at least and what better way to spend an evening. Many of the rooms were in individual chalet type accommodation and we had an air conditioned family chalet. Each day they left us fruit juice and a bowl of fruit including freshly chopped passion fruit and coconut chunks, delicious on a hot day. The centre piece of the hotel and gardens was their famous sea horse shaped swimming pool. We spent our time there most days and mum read her books, dad played boisterous swimming pool games with us as he loved to do. It got very hot after midday and our parents introduced us to the idea of a siesta for an hour or two back at the chalet and much to our objection on the first day or two but I guess it was wise. You could live with having to take a mid-day siesta on a holiday like this one.

Given the great time we had every day, we made only one or two day trips out from the Smugglers Inn in Madang. One was out to sea in a small motor boat which Dad hired for a fishing trip one morning. We left quite early from the hotel and watched the local fishermen sail out before us. They paddled out with their children on board, one after the other in their hollowed out canoes, out into their calm bay. The canoes had wooden beams lashed to the long wooden floats which sat out on one side for balance. We hired the small motor boat for the morning with some instruction from the boat guy on how drive it and also advice on where and where not to go in the bay. Once we were out to sea a little, dad let me drive the boat by taking the wheel and the throttle handle just like the guy had showed us. I guess he was showing my dad, not me but as I say, my dad let me drive the boat! The boat also had fishing rods on board and we chopped up squid to bait the hooks. We trawled the lines off the side of the boat an also tried dropping the bait deeper but didn't catch any fish. It didn't matter, I was driving a motor boat around in the beautiful bay off the coast of Madang. *"Swing back around that island over there son, keep it nice and steady above the coral reefs."*

The blow hole
In Madang we made one other fabulous day trip, along the coast road leading north east in a hire car. Out to sea we passed more than one volcanic island, which were known to be active at times. They were large and unmistakable, smoking from the top of their perfect volcanic shape and lying a few miles off shore in the bright blue/green Bismak Sea. We travelled along beautiful coast road which had only occasional houses and villages on the land side and made it's way through plantation after plantation of coconut and banana palms. As ever in Madang it was very hot, we were looking out to sea where the equator lay only a few hundred miles off shore

The North Coast Road, madang

There was also a destination in mind, an intriguing sounding place called the *blow hole*. This seemed the only real recommended trip as some local people had spoken of it in an almost legendary way. The fact that we didn't know the exact location of the blow hole only added to the adventure. It was maybe thirty or so miles up along the north coast. The heat of the journey prompted us to stop at a motel for cold drinks, Fanta and Coca Cola as always, from a refrigerator. It's never tasted quite as good to us since PNG. The motel was clearly a bit run down, it felt like it had been built the decade before in the sixties but maybe never quite taken off. There was no water in the swimming pool I remember that for sure. It was here we asked again about the blow hole and the owner gave us an idea where he was fairly sure it might be. We drove north again on the ongoing search. There were no sign posts for the blow hole, you just needed an idea of where to drive off the main cost road onto a track towards the sea.

The Blow Hole with volcanic island offshore

We didn't find it straight away and were all out of the car looking when Dad shouted he thinks this is maybe it! It was a large and very nicely formed rock poll, maybe two or three times the size of the hotel swimming pool. The waves came against the rock wall and blew through in places causing jets of sea water to spout high in the air. You might have been tempted to ask what the fuss was about, until you fitted your snorkel and mask and swam out above the corals. It was worth the journey in every sense. The Corals which lined the floor and walls were of intense red and orange and purple colours and crept out in wonderful shapes and branches everywhere in the pool. The shoals of tropical fish abounded above and in and out of the corals. The fish were of almost every colour imaginable and the most spectacular thing was that all the same coloured fish shoaled together. They danced and flashed in all directions as they swam to and fro in the currents.

Dad had figured out that the currents were created by a couple of underwater holes in the rock wall where the waves funnelled through from the other side. These holes he reckoned weren't big enough for larger predators to be able to come through. So here it was, the most amazing natural aquarium you could ever hope to swim in. To this day I sometimes talk about it with my brother and sister and all we can say is *"remember the blow hole"* It's not so much a question, just a case of *"remember the blow hole!"*

Madang was just fantastic in the early 1970s, especially the luxury we found at the Smugglers Inn compared to living in a basic house on stilts in Kerowagi high school compound. We were just a little sorry to have to leave the Smugglers Inn but eventually set off for the airport to fly back south into the Highlands. We arrived back at the airport and soon enough, fuel was being pumped into little Cessna aeroplanes, by hand pump from the fuel drums on the tarmac. Our pilot approached us and asked if it would be OK if we flew back to Kundiawa with him and a trainee pilot. I remember a brief chat between our parents but the answer was yes, fine as long as the qualified pilot was with him. I think our parents were just in the swing of things by this time, maybe the influence of their new Aussie friends was helping, but why not. "Trainee pilot, he has to learn some time?"

So the Madang trip is nearly over, we're airborne and we're flying back across the huge Bismark mountain range and heading back for the famous Bismark Gap. A real adventure and still going well but what now, they couldn't find it! We were up and down valleys in and out of clouds and skirting the hillsides but for quite a while it became apparent that our pilots couldn't find the Bismark Gap. Maybe the qualified guy had switched off a little as he was watching the trainee going through his routines but we were somehow off course and it was starting to give us all some cause for concern. At last though, *"there it is!"* said the qualified guy and he was pointing way up through the clouds. We clearly hadn't ascended enough into the usual path but now we did. We ascended sharply upwards with the propellers roaring, through a gap in the clouds and over we went, over the famous Bismark gap. To the relief of everyone, we were now descending again with our ears popping in the rapid drop in altitude and safely homewards. Finally, along the Chimbu river valley and a climb and hop upwards, onto Kundiawa airstrip, no drama!

I dont think you'd ever class our trip to Madang a package

deal, not by any measure. It was one week trip planned by our parents day to day to include some premium excursions at little extra cost. It had everything you'd want from a holiday in Papua New Guinea, with some dare devil excitement thrown in for free!

CHAPTER 7 - SCHOOL IN KUNDIAWA

After our holidays in Madang, we travelled home from Kundiawa to Kerowagi on the same road which we travelled to and from School every day. The same road trip we'd made on our first day arriving in Chimbu District. It was a seventeen mile trip as we used to tell our school mates and along the Chimbu highway as it was being upgraded for better access to the western Highlands. Most of the time the main highway was OK but is was surfaced with gravell and stones. On the newly graded surfaces we made good progress, in other places it was very rough. When you turned north at the Koronigl bridge and home for Kerowagi, the road could present all kinds of problems. Flooding, regular land-slides and tribal waring were some of the obstacles but there was also the long-long boy. I remembered him just now as I was writing. "Long-long" is pigeon English for anything from mentally unstable to positively insane. He lived in a village about half way between the main highway and Kerowagi, in a small completely traditional village with pit-pit bamboo huts with smoke filtering from the grass roofs. You'd occasionally see him shouting or throwing things at passing trucks and on one occasion we encountered him lying right in the middle of the road waiting for oncoming traffic. He was known to do this and you had to drive carefully around him or try to get help to move him. There were many examples of villagers having to cope with roads and trucks now coming through their territory. For the long-long boy though, his antics were maybe just one of his ways of passing the day.

The road from the Koronigl bridge to Kerowagi

Kundiawa was quite a bustling town compared to Kerowagi. It was near the meeting place of the Waghi river and Chimbu river valleys. Our dad took us along a road to look for the confluence of the two rivers one day, he was keen on confluences. We looked down on it from a hillside on the outskirts of the town, the two largest rivers in the Western Highlands coming together. Back home in Scotland we often passed the confluence of the river Ettrick and the river Tweed near where dad came from in Selkirk. He would always point it out, without fail *"Look down there kids, there's the confluence of the Ettrick and the Tweed"*

Our school was called "Kundiawa Primary A School". I think the "A" may have stood for Australia to differentiate it from the local Schools. It was for expatriate children meaning children from all "Ex Pat" families and only a handful of children from wealthier local Papua New Guinean families who I remember as Patrick and Nombri Yomba, Reva Nau and Nau-Dona. Nau was from Papua in the south as his name suggested, he had the more gentle features of the Papuans. He was the fastest guy in the school, a heck of a runner on sports day. One day the kids from two other primary "A" schools Minj and Bans schools from elsewhere in Chimbu came to Kundiawa rugby ground for much awaited inter schools sports. Naudona was our main guy for most events. He was a bit distraught in the morning because he didn't have proper sports shorts. One of our teachers, Mrs Gotts, had heard about Nua's concern and went off to the Steamships Trading and bought him a new pair during break time. In the main long distance race at the end of the day Nau-dona waited his time for the first few laps. With a couple of hundred yards left he took off and left them all in his wake. He came storming home forty or fifty yards ahead in his cracking new white sports shorts with the two red stripes on the side!

The other children at our school were mostly Australian and some of Chinese and German descent. I remember almost all of their names so I won't list them but they were not actually very easy to make friends with at first. Many of their parents were pioneering people working on road building projects and other frontier stuff and they made little allowances for anyone new. They had no airs & graces is another away to put it. On our first day at school I had the misfortune of having been sick in the back of the truck on the way from Kerowagi. Once one of us was sick on the journey, the rest seemed to follow. Anyway it meant that the first real greeting I got from classmates was *"Jesus you stink of bloody sick mate"* Also on that first day they took delight in realising we were Scottish and by around lunch time some classmates had launched into song.

> *"Edinburgh Castle, sits upon a rock,*
> *Anyone that passes has to show their cock,*
> *Lemonade an' soda sitt'n in a glass,*
> *If you don't like it, stick it up you arse!"*

Charming, what a welcome and by the way *"your packed lunch looks pretty shit mate"*. That's one endearing thing about Australians though, they always call you mate!

Six children travelled from Kerowagi to Kundiawa primary "A" school every school day. In the first year it was us three Lintons, the two Cisserra sisters Marie & Cathy, and Charlie Ariston junior, son of Charlie senior who was headmaster at Kerowagi high school. In the second year the Cisserras were gone and Charlie's younger brother Eddie joined us together with Elisabeth "Izzibet" Paterson. The parents all took turns to drive the 17 mile trip to Kundiawa and back every day. All sorts of vehicles made the trip including the public works department truck when required. Charlie used to show up sometimes in his Volkswagen Beetle car and squeeze us in. In the rainy season he drove that car though the mud-slides shouting *"we'll slice through it like butter"* as the engine roared from behind us as we sat packed together in the back seat. On one occasion when we had the school minibus, Cathy decided to get naked. Her sister Marie then reported this to her parents saying we were all making love on the bus. This meant an awkward conversation when Mr Cisserra showed up at our house that evening. Our dad agreed to deal with things and quizzed us at some length to establish that Marie's idea of making love was nothing more than Cathy's desire to get naked and throw her clothes around. Later that night our dad decided to tell us all about the birds and the bees to help us all with a better understanding, maybe also in the hope Mr Cissera wouldn't come banging on our door again.

Izzibet's dad was Bob Paterson who was manager at the PWD garage in Kerowagi among other things. Bob was the guy who supplied us with large inflatable inner tubes from truck tyres which we used to tumble down the rapids on the Koronigl and Chimbu rivers. We called this practice *"gummying"* and we held on tight but bumps and injuries were unavoidable. Izzibet was a bright spirited girl, a very welcome addition when she joined us on these trips and she loved to sing songs on the long drive to and from school.

> *" Liddle red caboos,*
> *Liddle red caboos,*
> *Liddle red caboos behind the train,*
> *Rumblin' down the track,*
> *Smokestack on his back,*
> *Liddle red Caboos behind the train!"*

The school building itself was well appointed, it stood on stilts like most of the newer style buildings to protect from floods in the rainy season and had a nice symmetry about it. There were two classrooms with two stairways leading up like an inverted 'V' shape to the two classroom doors which sat side by side in the middle. On the platform at the top of the stairs a water cooler sat in the shade against the wall. The school was on higher stilts than for most buildings and we were able to play in the area under the classrooms on rainy days. Our favourite game was floor hockey which led to quite a few injuries. Our brother Roger was in the younger class for 5-8 year olds and my sister Janet and I were next door in the older class. Tough on Rog being on his own but he had a good pal early on called Nombri Yomba and then another great friend arrived called Warwick whose dad was a foreman on the Highlands Highway. I could write another whole chapter about Warwick's family, they sure lifted things for Rog. Warwick's dad seemed to spend much of the time roaring out *"Warwiiiick!"* as he and Rog tore down a track into the bush on Warwick's motorised go-kart!

The school was up the hill out of town to the south of Kundiawa and looked over the town itself to the mountains on the north side of the Chimbu valley. Looking across the town, you could see a road snaking up the hill to the Luthern mission where Jenny Houter lived. There were actually quite a few kids at school whose parents were involved in missionary type work. Katy Langbrook was from a Jehovah's Witness family. In the second year we attended, Mr Littley arrived as the new headmaster with his family who were also Jehovah's Witnesses. This was a feature in PNG at the time, missionaries from the various religions were there looking to spread their own faith in this recently discovered territory. To be fair to Mr Littley, he didnt push any religeous things our way but we noticed the little things. Toy guns were expressly banned from school by Mr Littley and Katy Langbrook let us know their families didn't accept any presents on her birthday or at Christmas time. She was a great fun girl though Katy she was unabashed and liked to joke about all things. My sister Janet and her friends had decided to give Katy birthday presents regardless. Katy arrived at school the next day to say she'd hidden the bars of cholate under her skirt as she approached the road to her house, only for the chocolate to melt in her nickers by the time she reached her bedroom!

Singing was really great in the first year at the school. Our teacher and headmaster Mr Ron Denholm accompanied the singing on his guitar. As well as lots of traditional Aussie songs, Ron was teaching us some contemporary songs by the Beach Boys, Cat Stevens and the Beatles and he had us singing the harmonies, it was the best part of my day. Could I imagine Mrs Rutherford back in Scotland singing a Beach Boys song with the class, not likely!

> *"The kukabara sits in the old gum tree,*
> *Merry merry king of the bush is he,*
> *Laugh kukabara laugh kukabara*
> *Gay your life must be"*
>
> *"We came on the sloop John B,*
> *My grand pappy and me" etc.*
>
> *"I'm being followed by a moon shadow*
> *Moon shadow, moon shadow*
> *Leaping and hopping on moon shadow*
> *Moon Shadow moon Shadow*
> *If I ever lose my legs*
> *I wont moan and I wont beg*
> *If I ever lose my legs,*
> *I wont have to walk no more ..."*

Cat Stevens – Moon Shadow, a favourite song.

In class we studied the Australian curriculum including the expected reading and writing elements. Reading progressed through a series of colour coded books called SRA readers. These troubled me personally as my slow progress in reading in Scotland continued just as slowly abroad. If it hadn't been for the colour coding system it wouldn't have been so obvious but a cover up would probably also have been unwise. I struggled on, with my orange SRA reader at my desk, in the knowledge that it was more common in the younger class next door. The rest of the class moved on through red and purple and I think maybe silver and gold. A tough moment came when Rog caught up with me on orange but I think they helped me onto the red reader book soon after and that felt fine!

We also learned the geography of the region and could draw maps of PNG, Australia, Tasmania and the Soloman Islands. David Chee was the best at drawing maps, his were excellent. He could place West Australia, the Northern Territories, Queensland, Victoria and New South Wales perfectly with all their capital cities in place. I can still make a good attempt at this but my maps were never as perfect as those drawn by David Chee. One other thing we learned was scale drawing where you placed a scaled grid on top of a cartoon. You then repeated the grid on larger scale on a much larger piece of paper and filled in the boxes. This then gave you an excellent scale up of the cartoon and we amazed ourselves once we coloured in all in the boxes. I've taught this technique to my own children and we produced some excellent giant cartoons. I'm not sure if they taught things like scale drawing in primary schools UK back then, popular mainly in the highlands of Papua New Guinea?

In the playground our main play stuff had been provided by the Dillinger Highways Company where some of the pupils' parents worked and took the form on a climbing frame with some ropes and a very large truck tyre which I remembered at the mention of David Chee. David was small and slender enough to lie inside the truck tyre and he was the one guy brave enough to let us roll him around for one or two revolutions of the massive tyre. On one notorious day though, we managed to lose control of the tyre and it rolled from the play ground level, off down the terraced hill and eventually into the bushes next to Mr Littleys house! We ran to get him out of the tyre and he emerged pretty shaken. He was so dizzy and disoriented he had to lie on the ground for a while with a drink of water. He insisted no-one summon the teachers though and by the time he was back up the hill, he was the proudest guy in school!

Justin Fisher and his parents lived on the hillside above the school, one house up from the McIndoe brothers. He was an avid stamp collector, with his parents help and soon he had us all into collecting stamps. Thanks to Justin's enthusiasm, I have a great little stamp collectors book where the stamps chronicle the events of the time including the proposed set up of a television station to broadcast around the Port Moresby area. During the writing of these memoirs I set out to find my stamp collection and after many hours of searching I found it in a tied up bag of maps in a storage box in the garage. I'd been through all the boxes several times and had very nearly given up on finding the collection. I'm delighted to have found it as it forms an interesting postscript to this memoir for anyone interested in stamps and what they tell us from the time.

The next building up the hill from our school was a small catholic mission. In the mission garden there was a large mango tree and shortly after the start of our time at the school, the mangos ripened. We climbed up and picked them with other kids from the school which wasn't really allowed as it turned out but the large stones and skins discarded in our school playground gave the game away very quickly. Very occasionally, the priest from the mission was invited into the school to give us some local history lessons. He didn't tell us anything religious as far as I remember but had been in the area for quite a few years and he had fantastic things to tell us. He asked if we'd seen how many of the native men often wore bones through their noses on ceremonial days and of course we had all noticed. He explained that every tribe had a medicine man as he interpreted it, each dialect had a different name for him. Custom dictated that the medicine man had a small house on a bridge above the river.

"Did he live in the house? we asked.

"No not all the time but that's where he practiced medicine and there was a reason the medicine man's house was always above the river"

The priest explained that when young men came of age they went to the medicine man's house. It was here that he took a very sharp poker and pierced the young men's nose at the septum. They could be heard to scream and then the blood was allowed to run through a hole in the floor and into the river below. This meant that the young mens' mother's blood had now left their body. A piece of boiled pig bone was then inserted in the hole in the young man's nose and when he emerged from the house above the river he was now a man. That evening, the village would have a celebration of coming of age. When things healed up around the bone the hole was now there for good and bigger better bones could be inserted over time, the biggest and best being kept for ceremonial occasions.

I used to look forward to the priest's visits and the things he passed on to us. He also told us all about the early explorers, some of whom he had known. They had made their way into the highlands on single bush tracks with packs on their backs and and armed with shotguns *"but they came in peace"*. They camped where they could and brought gifts for the natives to help befriend them. Sadly, I can't remember the priest's name or many of the other things he told us but what a fantastic guy. He never once complained about us stripping his tree of mangos. That's the one story I was bound to remember, about how the men of the highland villages came to wear the bones in their noses.

CHAPTER 8 – KEROWAGI HIGH SCHOOL

Our parents loved their time in Papua New Guinea. As I explained earlier they had already spent the best part of one year teaching in Nigeria in 1965 just after Roger was born. Unfortunately we had to return home unexpectedly to Scotland due to the break out of the Biafran war. This only enhanced their taste for adventure however and may have helped them accomodate the twist of fate which took them to the Western Highlands rather than the intended tropical paradise of Manus Island. In Kerowagi High School they met like-minded people and lifelong friends. Only a few weeks ago our mum mentioned needing to catch the overseas Christmas post to Joan Graham and John Pickles in Australia.

They had a challenging job on their hands as there was a real variety of children attending Kerowagi High School. They travelled from all over the highlands to board there in the large basic dormitory buildings. There were no other Schools of this type from Goroka to Mount Hagen, Kerowagi may have been chosen or its fairly central location in the Western Highlands. High school pupils whose parents could see the need for education sent them there from far and wide and many of the pupils were there thanks to their own determination. This meant for a very progressive school environment as far as I remember. These young people knew they were privileged to be there where others were less fortunate and knew the value of education. Their gradual exposure to the infux of other cultures in PNG now generated real appetite for learning. Our parents and the other pioneers were charged with teaching them English, Maths, Languages, sports, history, geography, home economics and farming. There was a farm within the school campus where ducks, pigs and chickens were reared. They also gave the students an insight into the world beyond the Western Highlands of PNG. They did this without the aid of television or any visual aids back then and with the aid of only books and their own teaching skills.

For all of the staff, keeping discipline day to day was also a challenge considering Kerowagi mas a mixed sex boarding school. Our dad seemed to be at the centre of much of this activity and he set up a discipline system called the punishment book. It was actually brought home with us along with the album of photos Mr John Blacksland gave us as a gift. Pupils names and misdemeanours are listed day to day together with an allocation of hours to be spent on work parade depending on the nature of each offence. In any given week there can be forty to fifty offences listed against named individuals by members of staff. Those which recur the most involve taking food from the mess hall, causing disturbances after lights-out, going out of bounds, forgetting spades for field class and failing to show up for work parade itself. Here are a selection of other offences which help to illustrate some of the challenges faced in the school at the time:

- *Dangerous use of a grass knife*
- *Swifting from Dorm to Dorm*
- *Hiding a bucket of tea*
- *Entering the mess room kitchen to steal bananas*
- *Ran off in fear and shame to Kundiawa, stayed for two days*
- *Violence, causing injury with scissors*

- ❖ *Philandering in Kundiawa during home leave*
- ❖ *Playing ukulele after lights out*
- ❖ *Sewing shorts after lights out*
- ❖ *Playing table tennis during library period*
- ❖ *Flea hunting during library period*
- ❖ *Making a bilum bag during library period*
- ❖ *Dipping a burning stick in the dish washing copper*

Interestingly, a high proportion of the offences and misdemeanours were recorded during library period. Like in any school in the world I guess, library period was used for many and varied purposes, aside from reading. It's also clear in many cases that the adolescent boys at the school landed in trouble regularly for going out of their way to impress the girls. The girls often reacted by looking scornfully at them during many of these attempts and using the expression *"Wat' are yooou?"* and also *"Look at yooou!"* It's another one of these things which stayed with our family over the years and we regularly put each other down with *"Wat' are yooou!....Look at yooou!"*. In Scotland it translates to something like *"Who d'ye 'hink ye are?"* . Written out neatly in the front pages of the album of photos John Blacksland gave us is a poem by one of the senior girls, which he may have asked her to write into the album. It gives an insight into the way our dad was seen in his role at the school which wasn't an easy one at times and contains these popular expressions of the time.

A poem – Mr John McLinton (Great English Expresser)

Mr John McLinton,
What are you,
A man full of English Expressions
A man full of English Jokes
On what are you,

Aren't you lucky to be born with these things

Oh what are you
Mr John McLinton
A man full of dramatic expressions
A man full of dramatic actions
Oh what are you
Aren't you lucky to be born with these things

Oh what are you, Mr John McLinton,
A man full of stories,
A man full of jokes,
A man full of laughter,
But he is also a man full of anger,
When he is annoyed at the boy,
He poured words of expressions after expression,
And the boy sits, with head down

Oh what are you, Mr John McLinton
A man full of history stories,
A man full of jokes,
A man full of Scottish histories,
Oh what are you,
Aren't you lucky to be born with these things.

Elizabet Tongia, 4E, 1974

Going missing from school or returning a few days late from home leave is also a very common entry in the punishment book. There was a real desire for education among the pupils but this was balanced against the pull of the tribal culture from which they all came. Our mum was the mistress for the large girls dormitory next door to our house on the school compound. Some years ago she told us a story at dinner about the time she went to the rescue a girl called Irmgard from her village. I asked our mum Mary if she might write the episode down for us and here it is, to share with you:

How Irmgard Escaped Unwanted Matrimony!

Kerowagi High School had a policy of granting students home leave on the last week-end of every month from Friday lunch time till Sunday evening. By Wednesday I realised Irmgard hadn't returned. As mistress in charge of girls, I inquired if anyone knew why. I was told she was being kept back in her village by her brother who wanted "bride price", a custom practiced then and perhaps to this day. Irmgard would have been around fifteen to sixteen years old. Few of the pupils knew their exact age. I knew her father worked and lived in the catholic mission so I went to ask him if he knew and approved of the arrangement. He told me he certainly did not but he was rather an older father and I could tell he was afraid of the son. However, he agreed to my getting Irmgard back to school if I could. A young man who was standing nearby offered to take me to the brother's village. This involved driving back off the highway along forest paths then walking along a muddy path for around five minutes.

On arriving at the village we were immediately surrounded by a group of young men amongst whom was the brother. I explained that I had come to get Irmgard and that I had her father's permission to take her back to school. At this point, Irmgard appeared from one of the huts. She was completely her village self, face painted, bare breasted, grass skirted, looking rather different. I explained again I had her father's permission to take her back to school if that was what she wanted. She confirmed it certainly was and off we set followed by this group of muttering young men who seemed to get closer and closer as we rounded a bend and saw the car. Irmgard at my side just kept muttering "Oh missus, missus!" I was feeling a tad nervous myself. I have to admit we practically ran the last dozen yards to the car, jumped in, banged the doors and bumped our way back down onto the highway. There was silence for the first ten to twenty seconds then Irmgard burst into giggles. "Oh missus, oh missus ayee! ayee!". I took it she was pleased.

Mary Linton, January 2020

We were fascinated to hear that story, thankfully we're a family who sit long at dinner and exchange memories such as these. Mum also mentioned that dad had been initially quite concerned about her having done this at the time but she explained to him he'd been busy so she decided to go herself. She admits now it was maybe quite a dangerous thing to have done but I suspect that at the time, she knew her way might be the best. It was a daring plan, we can say that much, it most probably changed the course of young Irmgard's life from that day onwards.

In general things went very well at Kerowagi High School but one thing remained clear, the tribal world the pupils grew up with was ever present. This presented another challenge at times as they would rally together quite effectively if they felt ill done by. Some of the young guys had been brought up knowing they were destined to be tribal chiefs hence there were often rivalries and uprisings in the school. On one occasion, our dad being a figure of authority came into conflict with a crowd of pupils who were armed with spears and axes ready to march on our house. We got the help of the local Kiap Bill Graham who arrived in his truck and armed with his shotgun to help talk down the rebel group.

For the students, there were a lot of activities outside of the classroom to add to the overall entertainment. Our parents were heavily involved in school plays which were presented in the school hall on the main drive. The pupils loved taking part and the audiences screamed and laughed at the antics on stage. There were occasional dances where records were played by bands such as the *New Guinea Copy Cats*. Their big hit was a cover version of B*eautiful Sunday*. On one occasion, Rog and I were going down the hill to the creek to dig out some clay on a Sunday morning and we could hear the Singing as we approached. The girls' dormitory next to our house took the same path to the creek. A group of seven or eight girls were showering and shampooing under the waterfall and singing....

> "This is my, my, my beautiful Su-un-day
> This is my-my-my beautiful day-ay-ay
> When you say, say, say, say that you lo-ove me
> Oh-oh oh my, my, my it's a beautiful day."

They screeched and fussed a little as we approached but then they just carried on showering and singing! The clay bank of pristine blue clay was situated right next to the waterfall as it happened. The incident was mentioned to our mother who was patron of the girls' dormitory and we were warned not to disturb the girls in future. We weren't seen as same the threat the high school boys, they could be disciplined or suspended for disturbing the girls privacy but we were warned not to go down to the waterfall on Sundays again. I confess I'm still reminded of the scene at the waterfall when I've heard that song in the many intervening years ... "*This is my, my, my beautiful Su-un-day!*"

The other thing our parents brought to the school was

Scottish Country Dancing. They'd take the record player to the school hall, co-opt a few fellow teachers into the venture and started up Scottish Country Dance evenings. They had a couple of Scottish Country Dance LP records which we didn't actually play much in our house. You wouldn't believe how popular these nights became, an instant hit with the pupils. They quickly learned the *Dashing White Sergeant, Eight-some Reel, Gay Gordons and Strip the Willow.* Our Dad's announcement to get ready for each dance began to be met with cheers and screams each time and they went at the dances with huge enthusiasm. In Scotland people occasionally let out a hee-uch shout during a dance, the schoolkids screamed and roared throughout and soon had the dances off to perfection. They danced in their bare feet and a dust cloud rose in the hall, even after best attempts to sweep it before the dancing. So there's how Scottish Country Dancing arrived in Chimbu District, Western Highlands Papua New Guinea, in 1973.

On one day each year the school had a national celebration day and excitement really grew as the day approached. In the morning Father Fisher went to shoot a cow in the farm at the north end of the school compound. We watched from a distance, hiding behind the school mess hall in case we weren't supposed to be there. He put the gun at the back of the cow's head and it dropped straight to the ground then a fraction of a second later we heard the bang. The cow was then taken to the "mou-mou" feast. Large pits had been dug in the ground and stones were being heated in a bonfire nearby. My brother Rog and I then watched from a vantage point in a nearby tree as some local men and schoolboys then went about butchering the cow. They literally chopped it down its breast bone then used large poles to prise it open. Thankfully we weren't close enough for me to give you any of the gorier details but three stomachs emerged which was pretty surprising. When the heart was removed there was a lot of consternation at it was still twitching and beating. The many cuts of meat were then put into the large pits which were lined with banana tree leaves and the roasting hot stones were put in with them. The pits were then covered with more banana tree leaves and thus the meat was left to cook for the feast.

Pupils at Kerowagi High School in their National Dress

The students made a huge effort in the days running up to the national celebration to prepare their own national dress. They came from their dormitories looking incredible and looking extremely proud. In groups here and there they danced and chanted as they made their way towards the assembly ground and the mou-mou feast at the far end. They also performed a display of a courtship ritual called "karim lek" which was like a kind of kama sutra ritual. The teaching staff spent a lot of their time trying to ensure as few as possible carnal activities occurred between the sexes at the school. It was strictly forbidden but on the day of the national celebration the karim lek was permitted in a limited way and for a display only. Who knows what may have gone on in the many hiding places in the school compound in the excitement of national celebration day!

Our Parents had great friendships with the other teachers Kerowagi High School. All teachers lived in basic houses on stilts within the school compound. There was a real feeling of togetherness among them and among the pupils, despite the occasional uprisings! Out of school hours our parents socialised with all the other teachers, arranging barbecues, evenings in and afternoons at each other's homes. On Friday evenings we gathered with a few of their colleagues and sang songs accompanied by our guitars.

Given there was no television and only a limited World Service on the short wave radio, we made most of our own entertainment. We did have that old record player and our parents' friends occasionally brought other records once the Seekers & Nana Mouskouri were all played out. A young teacher called Mark Carrol who I remenber as a hippy type guy taught us to play guitar and loaned us some of his record singles including Crocodile Rock by Elton John. We started with the cords D, A and G and our dad taught me calypso rhythm and now we were all rocking. The first song we learned with these chords was *Sloop John B* by the Beach Boys, closely followed by an Australian song called the pub with no beer.

> *"Well its lonesome away from your kindred an' all,*
> *By the campfire at night, where the wild dingos call,*
> *(Everyone: Howoooool!)*
> *But there's nothing more lonesome, morbid or drear,*
> *Than to stand at the bar, of a pub with no Beer...etc."*

On some week-end days I'd travel with my dad and a guy called Kevin Perrit on occasional golfing trips. Yes, golfing trips in the highlands of Papua New Guinea. We'd set off early morning along the western highway in the direction of Mount Hagen then turn south after a while for a small town called Minj. It seems incredible looking back but Minj had a nine hole golf course where I caddied the clubs round for my dad and Kevin Perrit into the heat of the day. The reward was cold beers, coca cola and lunch in the golf clubhouse followed by a game of snooker. The people who settled in Minj really had themselves organised back then, they seemed to be the well-to-do people of the Western Highlands. They also had a lawn tennis court where we went to see a tennis competition one day, an excuse for a real party and pic-nic for ex-pat people in the area.

Our parents and their fellow teachers had the time of their lives and to quote my brother Rog, *"they were at the height of their powers"*. As all teachers will attest, having class of pupils ready and willing to learn it what makes it worthwhile. They taught the students everything they could and opened their minds to new subjects and to the wide world beyond the Western Highlands. The period where overseas teachers provided this service was drawing to a close however, as New Guinea became independent from Australian government in 1974 during our time there. Their own newly installed government led by Michael Somare was now beginning to appoint teachers from among many young PNG natives already moving on and graduating. I think one main University was established in Port Moresby when we left PNG.

CHAPTER 9 - PNG A COUNTRY MOVING ON

In the two years we spent in Papua New Guinea in 1973/74, things were changing rapidly. The project to upgrade the Highlands Highway was in full swing all of that time. It brought with it access to hitherto remote areas in the highlands and allowed the highlanders much better access descending from their villages to rapidly growing towns of Goroka, Kundiawa and Mount Hagen. This meant progress but also meant for difficulties, one being safety and security on the new roads. In one incident a family in a dark green truck had run over and killed a child on the road near Goroka. A warning went out to any expats driving a similar truck to be very careful driving anywhere in the highlands at the time as some villagers had revenge in mind.

Road gangs also started to emerge including one organised gang named the Rascols. These gangs had many clever and devious ways of stopping and robbing travellers and trucks carrying increasingly prized products along the new highways. As with the Siku - Gena war already mentioned, tribes and villagers now fought over land for it's value in terms of commercial plantation as well as occupancy. In the capital, Port Moresby crime was on the rise. We heard news of areas where people in wealthier housing were starting to fence themselves in.

During 1974, her majesty the Queen of Great Britain & Northern Ireland & Prince Philip came to visit. The visit was to commemorate Papua New Guinea's independence from Australian and British rule. They laid on quite a party for the royals including huge tribal displays and the arrival of an elephant which the locals referred to as "bikpella pik" (big pig). We went down to the Highway to watch it passing on a truck, sponsored by who else but South Pacific Beer.

We often reminisce about our time in PNG. I've told many of these tales and episodes to many people over the years. Once people realise we were there, they're curious to know about it and we're always happy to tell. I guess the realisation of people's fascination also led me to write this memoir. I've written it in my 55th and 56th years but the memories are entirely through the eyes of a boy of nine and ten years old. What I recall of life in Scotland before going to Papua New Guinea seems mostly in black & white in my memory. What I recall of PNG is then entirely in colour and likewise when I return to Scotland its mostly black & white again. I can't entirely explain why the memory remains so vivid except that when your awareness is heightened, memories maybe lodge more firmly in your mind and especially when you're young.

To try to express my overall feelings about this adventure doesn't add any more to the tale. Our parents took on the challenge and from then on I don't think any of us realised the degree of adventure it would entail. The feelings and experiences came our way from the moment of first hearing the news in our bath tub, when Rog shouted Guinea pigs! The journey we went on to get there, to a very much different destination to the one we set out for. Going to PNG was definitely our parent's intention but changing course for the Western Highlands definitely wasn't. On reflection, missing the flight from London to Sydney, with all the ongoing delays which ensued was probably a real stroke of luck. There wouldn't be any tales of living in a tribal war zone if we'd ended up on Manus Island. We wouldn't have flown onto mountain runways which you approach from below rather than above, nor would we have taken on epic road trips through the highlands to the north coast of PNG.

We've never ventured back in the many intervening years, I'm still not sure if we'd want to. I do wonder about how things have progressed. Chimbu district is now called Simbu district I know that much but are there now even more luxurious hotels in Madang compared to the Smugglers Inn? Is the blow hole still there and undamaged and is the pub open again in Kerowagi? I doubt it in the case of the blow-hole but I hope so in the case of the pub and hope that the Siku and Gena people are now at peace?

As you'll have guessed we took off on six similar flights on our way home to Scotland in reverse order to those I described on the way. My only concern on completing this memoir would be that on focussing on the family adventure, I havent told you enough about the people of Papua New Guinea. On looking through the chapters however, they're there every time in some way. I loved the way they hollered down the valleys at sunset, their fantastic gatherings and all their unique customs. John Blacksland's photo of the Siku-Gena payback is possibly one of the most hitoric you'll see, and we were all there to witness it.

We flew home on a much superior Boeng 747 Jumbo jet aircraft compared to the Boeing 737 which we flew out on two years earlier. Three seats at one side, five in the middle and three on the far side. Not the same experience as flying over the Bismark Mountains in a Cessna with a trainee pilot at the helm though! Mum had bought us new Levi jeans in Sydney on the way home to the Scottish winter and the feeling of long trousers against my legs for the first time in two years felt very strange indeed. We landed back in a shiny new Edinburgh Airport with no resemblance to Edinburgh Turnhouse from which we'd left. It was a dark winter evening with all the street lights shining brightly above the tarmac roads and frost glistening on the pavements. We drove back to Musselburgh, directly through the city with the castle lit up beautifully against the night sky. "Edinburgh castle sits upon a rock...!"

I'm forever grateful for the experience. It has shaped much of my attitude to life ever since. As well as being grateful to our parents, we're proud of what they achieved. Proud of what they did for the young people of the Highlands of PNG, for themselves and for their children.

This is our flag, flag of our land
Proudly it flutters and proudly we stand
Flag of our Island, home in the sun
Papua New Guinea, we are one!

EPILOGUE

Recently at a family dinner I was asking whether my mum or sister had met anyone else who'd been to Papua New Guinea during the forty five years which have passed since our return to Scotland. As it happens, other than a few contacts our mum has kept from our time there, they haven't met a single person. My brother is in Malaysia with his wife and young daughter, spending two years teaching as it happens! By now he may have come across people who've been in PNG, it's only a cessna flight across the water.

I've met two people in the intervening time. I was working in a packaging company while studying in Edinburgh in 1981, seven years after returning. I was reminiscing with my boss in the laboratory about PNG and he took me to meet an elderly guy who was operating a rolling mill. He'd been in PNG as a young man in the 1930s during the Bulolo gold rush on the north coast. He explained that there weren't any gold mines as such but they were literally "hosing down mountains", as he put it. Every day they set up huge pumps which drew water from the sea. They then hosed and blasted the water against the mountainsides and they extracted the gold from the slurry which ran back down the channels. According to this elderly colleague, entire mountains gradually disappeared one by one around the town of Bulolo during these operations.

The other person I met was a guy I coached and played rugby with at our local rugby club. He now lives in Scotland but he's from New Zealand, a great rugby enthusiast as you'd expect. He went to work in Lae as a younger man as a manager in the coca cola factory. I told him about one of the most refreshing coca cola drinks I'd ever had, in the hotel bar right there in the town where he worked. He mentioned that it wasn't the best of times for him. In the 1990's working and living in Lae had become quite difficult and he'd head home as often as he could. By then he encountered a fair amount of crime in Lae and you weren't really free to go everywhere you'd ordinarily like to go. He also found it quite difficult managing the local workers in the factory. His story of his time in PNG is very different from the experiences of our family although it does have some parallels. This maybe reflects once again the rapid change the country was begining to go through during our stay in the early 1970's. It also echoes the changes described to us by our parents' friends who'd moved back to Australia. We're left with some sadness at hearing the ongoing difficulties PNG faced as it became more and more exposed to the culture of the developed world, without being in any way prepared.

PNG of course came to our notice over the intervening years in many other ways. Television documentaries about the Highlands and Islands of PNG have cropped up more regularly as the years have gone by. We never miss the chance for some insight as to how things are moving on. A tribe in the Sepic river delta who hunt crocodiles with their bare hands. A fantastic documentary capturing the diversity of the many species of birds of paradise and their amazing mating displays and rituals. It seems that in the more remote regions though, things haven't changed as quickly. Even in the 21st century, in large areas of PNG, people are still living a subsistence life.

The PNG rugby team is called the Kumuls and they now excel in the sport of rugby league. A ferocious side of very fit guys, they recently beat a Great British Lions touring side 28-10 in Port Moresby in November 2019. They're apparently the only country in the world where rugby league is their national sport. It was a night of great celebration in Port Moresby, I was waiting for the commentator to say "The South Pacific beer will be flowing in the streets of Moresby tonight!" I watch out for them coming on TV at every opportunity. This is the cracking badge from their kit and I'm on the look-out for a shirt, size medium. We sing their national anthem in the pub in Musselburgh sometimes if they're on the TV and we sometimes sing the PNG anthem just for the fun of it! Once you have Papua New Guinea in your heart, it never leaves you.

One other tale comes to mind in relation to the memoirs we've now recounted. I was in an auction house in a town called Bo'ness near where I live in Scotland a few years ago. During the day of the auction, people are free to browse everything in the auction room listed for the sale in the evening. I was taking a good look over an old style solid wooden chest of drawers and pulling out each drawer in turn, checking all the things a complete non expert thinks they need to check. An older guy had come right up next to me and was inspecting the drawers in turn as I drew them out. When we looked in the bottom drawer there were several football cards lying right at the back of the drawer. I've seen plenty of football cards in the time since I collected them as a boy and these were in very good condition, left in a chest of drawers from a house clearance. The fellow leaned across me a little and picked up one of the cards which I'm fairly certain was none other than John Greig and he says quietly *"he was a player in his day"*. He then slipped the card quickly into the inside pocket of his jacket. Incredible, in the same way the trip to PNG had interrupted my efforts to get my hands on John Greig, it actually happened again at the auction house in Bo'ness. As auction goers will know it's strictly forbidden to snatch anything at all during the viewing time and besides, all angles of the auction room are normally kept on camera surveillance. Of course I left the other cards in the drawer and closed it. If I'd had the chance, I might have lifted John Greig to take a closer look but I'd have put him back, I'm sure.

Postscript

Wanpela Taim Long PNG – Chronicle in Stamps

During the writing of these memoirs I was discussing with my sister Janet, some of the kids we went to school with in Kundiawa and we got to thinking back on why their parents were there in PNG. Most were involved in building the infrastructure, roads, hospitals, schools etc. Some were missionaries, some were teachers and in some cases we had a feeling they'd maybe been taking refuge in PNG for their misdemeanours back in Australia! I spent some time with a school friend at Kundiawa primary school called Justin Fisher, collecting and arranging stamps. Justin was an individual, a little off the wall and I liked him a lot. His parents were very nice people and I stayed overnight with them on one occasion, he lived very near our primary school. Many interesting things went on at the Fisher household such as collecting stamps and growing chillies in their garden. On passing the chilli bushes for the first time, Justin invited me to try one saying "they're just like sweets". They looked just like bright red jelly babies so of course picked one and proceeded to chew it. You can only imagine what I then went through, the Fisher's didn't just grow chillies, they grew the best! The only solace I could take from the experience was that Justin then went through a similar level of punishment and pain to what I'd been enduring.

As I also knew from Justin though, the Fisher family were

really avid stamp collectors. After dinner that evening Justin showed me their collection where they often bought full new issue sets of stamps called "first day covers" from the post office in display envelopes. After that visit I had my heart set on buying a stamp album and I bought a small one from the stationary section in *Steamships Trading* in Kundiawa. The stamps were all steamed from the airmail envelopes we received or in whatever way I managed to get my hands them on during our time in PNG. Many were also steamed from a large pile of envelopes & tear offs which Justin's parents had amassed and allowed us to pick through. We used tweezers to handle the stamps as advised by his parents so as not to damage the stamps with our fingers.

After making mention in the main text of these memoirs of collecting the four stamps commemorating the experimental introduction of television in PNG, I set out to find my PNG stamp collection. I had looked through our home and garage several times and searched my parent's home in Musselburgh. I searched the drawers in my old bedroom, our mothers many bookshelves and even the dusty boxes in the attic but to no avail. On what would have been a final search, I found my album camouflaged among my set of collectors maps in a storage box in my own garage. Given the historical interest of the set of stamps which formed the four corners of a television set, I wondered if the rest of the collection might also chronicle some of the events from our time in PGN in 1973 & 74. I'm pleased to say that they really do and not only during that time but well before our time there and a little after. For staying with me through these memoirs, I can only thank you for reading. If you stay on to look briefly at the modest collection of stamps, I thank you all the more.

On page one you can see the set of stamps commemorating the first television broadcast in PNG. If we look carefully on the post codes on many of the stamps on each page we can see when they were circulating, in this case 1973. I remember being overjoyed when I found the last stamp to complete the TV set and almost as much to see it again now. There's a stamp on the left of the TV set commemorating National Day 1972. The caption around the flag says "Bung Wantaim Ahebou - Unite" this literally means let's get together, in keeping with the recent joining together of Papua and New Guinea to form one nation. Next on page one there are stamps commemorating self-governance and one commemorating the young looking H.M Queen Elizabeth (2nd of England, 1st of Scotland) and Prince Philips' visit in 1974 marking the end of UK and Australian governance. There's a stamp commemorating the South Pacific games in 1971 and one showing some new coins due to be issued. The final stamp on page one commemorates Australia New Guinea Air services.

On page two the stamps depict PNG wildlife in the form of butterflies and birds of paradise are grouped together and again from the postmarks, all circulating between 1972 and 1974. These are fabulous just to look at but also for the record they read as follows:
Butterflies: Ornithoptera alexandrae and Ornithoptera victoriae regis.
Birds of Paradise: Pteridophora Alberti; Parota Carolae; Paradiseae Decora; Astraphia Mayeri.
In the case of Paradiseae Decora, the name maybe reflects the awkward fact that the feathers of this bird are very common in the headdresses seen in the photographs in

chapter 5. We must have the highest hopes that these species now have more effective protection and that they all still exist.

Page three shows a set of stamps circulating in 1972 &73 depicting regional aspects across PNG far and wide, including the some of the large islands which lie to the North. The islands of Bouganville, New Britain and Milne Bay are all there with the highly active volcano Mount Bagana on Bouganville. The regions and people on Central District, Western District and the East and West Sepic are also illustrated. On the same page, three stamps from another wildlife collection are also grouped.

Finally, on page four is a set of stamps which I didn't fully appreciate at the time of collecting them as a ten year old boy. (At the top of some pages you can see where I still haven't mastered facing all letters in the correct direction on the page) These are stamps which were circulating between 1973 and 1976 but actually commemorate much older stamps going back through the history of the island of PNG, i.e stamps commemorating stamps. One of the stamps is from a letter from Kundiawa we've received back home in Scotland in 1976 and forms part of this set. I must have steamed it off and added it to the collection. Fantastic! They show stamps from 1897, 1900 and 1914 entitled Deutsch Neu Guinea when Germany had a presence on the north Coast of PNG based in Rabaul, on the island of New Britain. The one we received back home in Scotland shows a stamp from 1901 entitled British New Guinea and finally a stamp from 1932 entitled only Papua from when Papua and New Guinea were separate countries.

128

Well, thank you Justin Fisher & family for introducing me to chillies & stamp collecting and providing me many of these stamps. It's been a real pleasure looking over them many years later. Each set of stamps was setting out to depict some key elements of PNG culture and the history and development of the country at this time. I hope we maybe meet again one day as I do for so many of the people we knew at the time in PNG. I'd say our efforts were worthwhile, providing a final glance at PNG history together with that stamp from Kundiawa we received back home in Musselburgh in January 1976.

ACKNOWLEDGEMENT

Thanks:
To Fiona and Logan McArthur for their continual encouragement to finish this book. To John Blacksland for the album of black & white photographs he presented our parents and Elizabeth Tongia for a poem therein. To our mother Mary Linton for "Freeing Irmgard". To Malcolm Mitchell for inspiration & to Andrew Gibb and Rod Hart for editing.

Printed in Great Britain
by Amazon